ICONS OF POPULAR CULTURE

Edited by

Marshall Fishwick

Ray B. Browne

Bowling Green University Popular Press
Bowling Green, Ohio 43403   USA

Library of Congress Catalog Card Number 73-127977
ISBN: 0-87972-003-4 Casebound
        0-87972-004-2 Paper
Printed in the United States of America.

ACKNOWLEDGMENTS

"Pop Icons," from *Art in the Age of Rock,* by Nicolas Calas, published by E. P. Dutton, Inc. (New York, 1968). Used by permission of author and publisher.

"Pop Iconology: Looking at the Coke Bottle," by Craig Gilborn, published in *Museum News,* December 1968. Used by permission of author and publisher.

Design on book adapted from *Museum News*, December 1968. Used by permission.

"Further Thoughts on Icons," copyright © 1970 by Marshall McLuhan.

The icon is for use,
when warm for prayer,
when cool for companionship.
—Nicholas Calas

Announcing a new series:

PROBINGS IN POPULAR CULTURE

These paperback monographs will investigate
new aspects of theory and practice in popular culture,
and old elements that need to be rethought and
restructured.

Even new fields quickly develop hard lines of
methodology, semantics, and content. Publishers and
journals understandably cater to the prevailing currents
and styles. Our series will probe and challenge, so that
early warning signals can be recorded and interpreted
in one of the fastest-growing areas of scholarship.

For further information, write either or both
of the co-editors:

Ray B. Browne
Bowling Green University
Bowling Green, Ohio 43402

Marshall W. Fishwick
Lincoln University
Lincoln Univ., Pa. 19352

CONTENTS

PREFACE TO SECOND EDITION

by

Marshall Fishwick

PREFACE TO SECOND EDITION

by

Marshall Fishwick

Whirl continues to be king. The world continues to change as we walk on it. Yet icons remain, and become ever more important in the global village. That, in a line, is our justification for expanding and re-issuing *Icons of Popular Culture.*

Let one example serve for the scores that could be presented. In the spring of 1972, *New York Times* reporter Hedrick Smith worked his way across Siberia, from Bratsk to Novosibirsk, to discuss the prospect of President Nixon's visit to the Soviet Union.[1] He found that it stirred little excitement. What fascinated Siberians were America's icons: her cars, clothes, and cokes.

In Irkutsk, for example, a taxi driver wanted to know more about American cars. A 23-year old Bratsk factory-worker and musician couldn't buy groovy clothes for his rock group: so they made them themselves. The beat goes on.

So does the epidemic of interest and research in the area of popular culture. A massive unprecedented cultural stock-taking is underway in the 1970's. The outlines of a new, post-European life-style have emerged: diffuse, unrefined, immature, baffling, sometimes banal—but multi-level, confident, vigorous, vital. "Help Wanted" signs are up all over the land. This is how they read:

WANTED: new reality forms, and ways to describe them for others.

WANTED: new ways of articulating actual structures of feeling . . . of unlocking meanings of life as it is actually lived.

WANTED: new ways to identify and describe the icons which form the visual center of modern life.

WANTED: sharp knives to cut through the blubber of our times—the academic dry rot, cliches, rhetoric and prerogatives that obscure reality.

This little volume, and others released in our "Probings in Popular Culture" series, are efforts to answer in part those want ads. Much more is wanted and needed. Our probings have only begun.

NOTES

[1] A full report was carried in the *New York Times* on March 30, 1972.

ENTRANCE

by

Marshall Fishwick

Icons are images and ideas converted into three dimesions.
They are admired artifacts, external expressions of internal convictions,
everyday things that make every day meaningful.

Icons are also cultural ciphers. They help us to de-cipher,
or unlock, the mystery of our attitudes and assumptions. As objects
they can be approached objectively; but people who believe in them
also operate on an emotional level—the level of love and reverence.
The real task for one who would fully appreciate icons is not merely
to define them, but to participate in the iconic life.

To do this one need merely to have a coke. . .thumb
through the Sears Roebuck catalog. . .pick up the telephone. . .drive
down to the corner drug store. Perhaps your car has a Virgin Mary

on the dashboard or had a St. Christopher before he was deposed—
artifact, image, symbol, icon— plastic Catholicism in the 1970's!
Thus do old and new icons converge in our driveways.

Pop icons are new and at the same time old. Of course
we do not admit being shocked by tradition. But what Papal decree
can take St. Christophers' medals from sophisticated jet travellers?
What college president dare order all amulets from around the necks
of Black Militants?

Icons accumulate and alter—but also lose—meanings.
The iconic Virgin Mary does not speak to the twentieth century as
she did to the thirteenth. The swastika does not motivate European
youth of the 1970's as it did those of the 1940's. Man carries
meanings, not merely objects invested with meanings. The image
precedes the idea in the development of human consciousness; but
the idea drives the image on to glory or oblivion.

In *Icon and Idea,* Herbert Read observes that "thinking
in pictures" is the first stage of icon-making. The ensuing steps
necessary to the construction of icons were taken as early as the
prehistoric period. All cultures invent icons. Freud spoke of "optical
memory-residues—things as opposed to words." The mind is not so
much a debating society as a picture gallery. We look with our eyes,
see with our minds, make with our hands. Form and formula fuse.
The word becomes flesh, and dwells among us.

The standard dictionary definition of icon (from the
Greek root eikon)—"an object of uncritical devotion"— does not
penetrate layers of meaning and emotion which cluster around it.
Icons are symbols and mindmarks. They tie in with myth, legend,
values, idols, aspirations. Because of the great stress religion places on
icons, some people would limit their icons to conventional religious
images typically painted on a wooden panel.[1] But such a restriction
is unrealistically narrow. We seek to revitalize the word and relate
it to popular culture. Icons still move men, even when they are not
recognized as such in supermarkets, discotheques, used car lots, and
funeral parlors. They pop up on billboards, TV commercials, and

magazine covers. Manna may still come from heaven; but much daily
fare flows through the Big Tube, which constantly flashes images
and cools outer reality.

Traditionally icons connote fixity and permanence;
but pop icons deal with the flux and impermanence of contemporary
Protean Man. A style of self-process and simultaneity is emerging;
icons, like everything else, adapt accordingly. Objects are the
building-blocks; ideas the cement holding them together. Modern
man is starved for ideas and objects that give coherence to electric-age
culture. What he finds most acceptable, Robert Jay Lifton notes, are
"images of a more fragmentary nature than those of past ideologies.
These images, though often limited and fleeting, have great influence
upon his psychological life."[2]

With all the changes icons are still omnipresent. The old
process continues: history becomes mythology, mythology begets
ritual, ritual demands icons. Concepts end up as creeds and icons.
Careers of men as different as Buddha, Christ, Marx, Einstein, and
McLuhan confirm it. In secular times religious icons remain. For
some they work; for others they have relinquished their power.
Diedrich Bonhoeffer, German theologian martyred in Hitler's Germany,
sensed this:

> Honesty demands that we recognize that we must
> live in the world as if there were no God. And this is
> just what we do recognize—before God! God himself
> drives us to this realization. He makes us know that
> we must live as men who can get along without him.

Millions live without much pain in a world where God
is dead. But we can't exist long without images. Living in the Secular
City, we crave and create a new physical and psychic environment.
In our time the icon goes pop.[3]

The tombs of Temples of ancient Egypt were full of icons.
There is a long unbroken history of sacred manna-bearing objects

throughout history. Christianity continued the use of iconography. "I have seen a great many portraits of the Saviour, of Peter and of Paul, which have been preserved up to our times," wrote Eusebius, Bishop of Caesarea in Cappadocia (265-340). The catacombs were icon centers, used by simple people as well as the ecclesiastical hierarchy. The meaning and language of icons was a major strength of Christendom for centuries. Old and New Testaments yielded up scores of symbols, themes, and inspirations; with every new saint new iconographic possibilities emerged. Key words were legend, belief, sacred object, veneration. Then and now icons are associated with age and class groups. They demand a cult, a lore, a spot of veneration. "All sacred things must have their place," Claude Levi-Strauss notes: "Being in their place is what makes them sacred. If taken out of their place, even in thought, the entire order of the universe would be destroyed."[4] What is central to the concept of icon is touching a center near man's essence. The content is the criterion of form.

By 1970 we have reached "Post Time"—post-modern, post-Freudian, post-Marxian, post-humanist: but not post-icon. Today, as in every epoch, men need to make sense out of the universe, in the context of time, place, belief. Even "natural" facts of birth, growth, and death are reacted to in a "cultural" fashion.[5] The style that develops is *sui generis,* of its own order. Former styles lasted for generations, even centuries; but in a single generation we have radically altered ours. The consequences are profound and traumatic, and demand unbiased study.

Instead of indiscriminate praise or damnation of popstyle (two current postures) we need to devise new criteria and categories for intrinsic meanings. Profiting from Erwin Panofsky's *Studies in Iconology* (1938), we should apply the same serious analysis to the current American Renaissance as was used for the older Italian and French. This would involve not only surface data (identification, description, authentication) but interior qualities (evaluation, interpretation, significance). It would also require an openness to popular culture which is notably absent in many parts of the academic community.

If this collection of essays shows anything, it is that there is no easy way to explain or proclaim the inner essence of popular icons. In the Age of Mass Man, meaning and response are still individual matters. Whatever each of us knows must be learned by each of us separately and in his own way. Your insight might be my oversight; your icon my kitsch. No mass media or external force can assure us of internal conviction. The operative word for icon is still *magic*.

This is not to say that our book points to a mystical experience. Icons, like all artifacts, are (among other things) visible and incontrovertible facts. They can be dealt with in space and time. Many can even be broken. Those who break them are iconoclasts.

Even the poorest among us has his private icon-bank. We make deposits there regularly, and withdraw more than we know. Just as we tuck away special treasures (notes, emblems, photos, medals) in the corners of drawers, so do we tuck away iconic images in the corners of our mind. We draw interest from our deposits. Icons have a way of funding us, and sustaining whatever sense and form our lives assume. When we can no longer draw from an icon bank, we quickly go bankrupt.

A hundred years ago Baudelaire invited fugitives from the world of memory to come aboard to seek the new. Subsequently there developed what Harold Rosenberg calls *The Tradition of the New* (1959). There have been few scholarly studies of it; few efforts to document Op, Cool, Retinal, Hard Edge, Post-Painterly Abstraction, LeNouvelle Tendence, Programmatic, and Psychedelic phases of painting, and simultaneous developments in other arts. Nor have the other items covered in this book received adequate attention. Statues are moving, movies are standing still. Films are reel illusion, and real life is more novel than fiction. The quality of feeling is intense but incoherent—like being thrust into Kubla Khan's psychedelic pleasure dome.

Iconologists must seek a point of significant beginning. This involves not only comparative study between arts, but configurational analysis of the total *gestalt*. Scholarship and criticism must catch up with performance. If today's poets and artists are (as they have always been) joint bearers of a central pattern of sensibility, let's find out what that pattern is. American Studies: begin here.

The mainstream of iconology in our time—because of its dissemination through mass media—is the popular stratum of our culture. The mechanized trivialized standardized world of which elitists complain provides the raw material for a new lifestyle. That pop artists have singled out objects for extensive use is an iconic clue. Ever since Robert Rauschenberg's 1958 "Coca-Cola Plan" that famous container, which Craig Gilborn calls "the most widely recognized commercial product in the world," has been featured. The history of soup cans was altered by Andy Warhol; no hamburger will ever be the same after Claes Oldenburg's pop depiction.

Coke bottles and soup cans are apt motifs not because they are unique, but because they are omnipresent. This means that, in the old traditional sense, they are anti-icons. Note how the nature of icons has changed between the Age of Faith and the Age of Atoms. The Coca Cola company jealously protects its trade mark and 1915 bottle design while putting those marks and bottles in every hamlet of the world. Pop icons are not only accessible; they are unavoidable.

Does it offend you to think that a TV tube, a Coke bottle, and a soup can feature in pop iconography? Are they not building blocks of the new Secular Culture? The Greeks had their Olympus; the Romans their triumphal arches; the Christians their shrines. Once these were all new— and "pop." Newness implies obsolescence of form and value; icons fade even as we venerate them.[6] Another name for the Holy Grail is New Style or New System. Putting the adjective "new" in front of a noun doesn't cancel connections with the old. The search for the new may indeed exalt the old. Camp Style of the 1960's suddenly put Victoria back on the throne, while

the film hierarchy was making room for two-bit Depression day
gangsters Bonnie and Clyde. Critics like C. Ray Smith now exalt
"the bold new poly-expanded mega-decoration" as we enter the
Age of the Nude Light Bulb. Simultaneously, a reprint of the 1897
Sears Roebuck catalog became a national best-seller. What are
Americans looking for in those pages of outmoded icons? What do
they find?

      Icons and symbols, like other fully operative and functional
parts of culture, tend to be assumed rather than defined by the people
involved. We are so used to seeing telephones, and the bell symbol
for the Bell System, that we forget the iconic importance of a revolutionary device. This irresistible intruder in time and place has introduced
what Marshall McLuhan calls a "seamless web of interlaced patterns
in management and decision-making."[7] Its power to decentralize
every operation has been felt but not understood by every business
and institution in the land. Whoever and wherever you are, the Bell
tolls for thee.

      The emblem itself, designed by Angus Hibbard in 1889,
went through four modifications before 1969, when the current one
was adopted:

Evolution of Bell Telephone Emblem Over Years

"We sensed that our symbols were losing their impact," said industrial designer Paul Bass when (in 1969) he gave "Ma Bell" her current model which now bedecks vehicles, uniforms, signs, letterheads, and hard hats. The switchover, involving 128,000 trucks, will take five years; how many millions of services the telephone— icon itself will perform in those years, how many life-and-death decisions will hum over its wires, no one can even guess.

Our communication systems, like many other things, mushroom faster than we can understand. If the corner store has become a supermarket, will we soon have super-icons? Not everyone approves of the proliferating aspect of popular culture. In fact, Benjamin DeMott foretells cultural pollution in *Supergrow:*

> Drifting sluggishly over the land from the
> international power struggle, a dense polluting wave,
> it penetrates the very marrow of the culture. Journalism,
> conversation, manners, the arts--the innermost thoughts
> and feelings of men—all are touched and tainted.[8]

But DeMott's regret is as weak as the paper barrier through which the Shell-powered car smashed. He would do well to remember that much of popular culture, like high fashion, is always ugly initially. Nothing that is unknown is accepted without a grimace and a fight. The nonsense of today is the truth of tomorrow; the truth of today the nonsense of tomorrow. This is what our eyes and cameras (Everyman's third eye) can verify. Speaking of the camera— is it a key icon of popular culture? Perhaps not, since as an instrument it *transmits* rather than *symbolizes* images. Not even photographers keep old cameras. The camera reaches its symbolic peak swinging from the necks of tourists around the world. But then it is an amulet rather than an icon—a charm which gives the wearer magic power.[9]

But surely the canvas or assemblage featuring the coke bottle, as well as the bottle itself, is an icon: an image converted into plastic form. Ideas like mass production, distribution, and taste become real in the three dimensional coke bottle (or canvas on which

it appears). Only in music has the validity of popstyle won wider
recognition than in art. Pop icons have been both identified and
enshrined (if we can borrow that sacred word for our secular culture)
by artists like Andy Warhol, Robert Rauschenberg, George Segal,
Robert Indiana, Claes Oldenburg, and Roy Lichtenstein. Theirs is
not the world of forests and wheat fields, but of automobiles, comic
strips, junk yards, and go-go girls. The whole apparatus of retail
emotions, gadgetry, and packaging is material for their art. They
exalt the thingness of things.[10]

"I am for art you can sit on," Claes Oldenburg writes.
"I am for the art of fat truck-tires and black eyes. I am for *7-Up Art,*
Pepsi Art, Sunkist Art. . .the art of tambourines and plastic phono-
graphs and abandoned boxes tied like pharaohs."[11] His subject
matter is pop iconography.

The most publicized young pop artist is Andy Warhol,
who has announced that he wants to be like a machine. Accepting
boredom and repetition, he piles up Brillo boxes to exemplify them.
His novel, entitled *A,* is a literal transcript of everything that happened
in a 24-hour period. Such performances raise the question what are
the boundaries of pop culture? What do the new icons signify?

The 1967 *Random House Dictionary* lists 21 meanings
for the verb "pop"—to say nothing of the noun, adjective, abreviation,
and link-words (popcorn, popeyed, popover, popgun, etc.) Pop is now—
faddish—in: the emphasis is on time. It's vernacular—folksy—earthy:
the emphasis is on place. It's universal—electronic—instant: the
emphasis is on technique. Pop is rooted in socio-economic factors
of our time: physical and social mobility, mass production, abundance,
anxiety. The definition itself is protean.

Space-time patterns have been affected. Our central
nervous systems have been extended into what Marshall McLuhan
calls "a global embrace." Action and reaction occur almost simultaneously. After 3,000 years of *exploding,* Western man is *imploding.*
We are all involved in one another's life. The icon flashes for thee.

As it flashes it confuses and sometimes enrages. The
arts seem to be a dialectic of outrage, an aggression on the audience.[12]
Many are capable of renunciation Rimbaud and Duchamp—or self

punishment—Holderlin and Artaud—or even suicide—Hemingway
and Gorky. The air is full not only of pollution but free-floating
resentment unleashed by cultural dislocations. We are turned on by
the energy of violence. . .the pop heard round the world.

Our contributors are Americans, but the icons they
describe jump national boundaries with ease. Pop icons are the best
known artifacts in the contemporary world. Kipling was wrong. The
twain *has* met; East and West swing together. No countries have been
so Americanized as Japan and Vietnam where observers note "spurting
sales of electric guitars, parlors and bowling alleys, and new-formed
hippie colonies."[13] This cultural borrowing is a two-way traffic.
Few forces have changed pop music as much as traditional sounds
from India.

Today pop icons are filling our landscape and forcing
channeling of our culture. They are the basis of the new reality. In
the Middle Ages all experience found philosophical unity and visual
form in a single metaphorical system. Will this be true in the 1970's?

This is only one of a series of questions which these
articles raise, but do not pretend to answer. In doing so perhaps they
serve as a microcosm of the newly-emerging field of popular culture.
Both "popular" and "culture" are words with multitudinous definitions
and overtones. There is a long-standing academic fear of "popular,"
which smacks of the vulgar, ephemeral, unscholarly, and (worst of all)
enjoyable. On the other hand, many practitioners of acknowledged
"popular" arts, such as comics or jazz scorn academic pomposity.
Thus Fats Waller to one seeking a definition of jazz: "If you don't
know what it is, lady, leave it alone!"

The essays in this volume are the result of hundreds of
letters and scores of conversations about a basic question: "What is
an icon?" No parameter occurred from those many definitions;
but a cluster of compatible words emerged—cipher, symbol, artifact,
emblem, amulet, totem, allegory, charm, idol, image. Friends urged
me to consult Erwin Panofsky's pioneering *Studies in Iconology*
(Oxford University Press, 1939), which begins by defining iconography
as "the branch of art history which concerns itself with the subject
matter or meaning of works of art, as opposed to their form." Then

follows an involved and abstract discussion on the distinction between meaning and form. Fourteen pages later we learn that the act of interpretation requires not only "pre-iconographical description (and pseudo-formal analysis) but iconographical analysis in the narrower sense of the word and iconographical interpretation in a deeper sense (iconographical synethesis)." The major thrust here is towards accurate description, with some attention to analysis. The synthesis is not yet in sight.

Other elaborate schemes for studying objects have been put forth recently by archeologists and anthropologists. The first essay, in which Craig Gilborn analyzes the coke bottle, follows this path. Some will find it most promising, from the viewpoint of methodology; others, too clinical and objective. They might prefer the belle-lettristic reminiscences of our senior scholar, Ben Botkin. Having published a piece on the Model-T Ford in 1930, he looks back over 40 years of interest in automania.

Botkin passes on the torch to his young colleague, Harry Hammond, a graduate student at the University of Delaware, whose "VW" is his first published essay. Hammond is back-to-back with Marshall McLuhan, the most discussed and contested figure in the area of mass media and messages. The "War of the Icons" which McLuhan describes continues—not only on battlefields, where weapons are icons, but in classrooms and seminars, breeders of both weapons and icons. If our collection serves as ammunition for some and target for others, our purpose will have been accomplished.

NOTES

[1] See, for example, Leonid Ouspensky and Valdimir Lossky, *The Meaning of Icons* (Basel, Otto Walter, 1952).

[2] Robert Jay Lifton, "Protean Man," *Partisan Review,* Winter, 1968, p. 47.

[3] Harvey Cox's study of *The Secular City* (New York, 1965) argues that Biblical faith desacralizes the cosmos. The sacred always goes bad unless it is working with the secular. For more on this theme, and the switch to pop, see Gibson Winter, *The New Creation as Metropolis* (New York, 1963) Larry Shiner, *The Secularization of History* (New York, 1966), Kenneth Hamilton,

What's New in Religion? (Grand Rapids, Mich., 1968), and Marshall McLuhan, *Understanding Media* (New York, 1964).

[4]Claude Levi-Strauss, *The Savage Mind* (Chicago, University of Chicago Press, 1969), p. 47.

[5]See Jerome Bruner, *Essays for the Left Hand* (Cambridge, Harvard University Press, 1963) and Elli Maranda, *Myth and Art as Teaching Materials* (Cambridge, Educational Services, Occasional Paper no. 5, 1965).

[6]For a fuller discussion see Louis Kampf, *On Modernism: The Prospects for Literature and Freedom* (Cambridge, M.I.T. Press, 1968).

[7]Marshall McLuhan, *op. cit.,* p. 234.

[8]Benjamin DeMott, *Supergrow* (New York, Dutton, 1969), p. 72.

[9]This notion was set forth by Beaumont Newhall, a leading historian of photography, in a letter to the author dated April 21,1969.

[10]See Mario Amaya, *Pop as Art* (London, Studio Vista, 1965) and Lucy R. Lippard, *Pop Art* (New York, Praeger, 1966).

[11]Quoted by Lucy R. Lippard, *Pop Art* (New York, Praeger, 1966), p. 106.

[12]Susan Sontag uses these phrases in *Styles of Radical Will* (New York, Farrar, Straus, and Giroux, 1969).

[13]See Emerson Chapin, "The Generation Gap in Japan." New York *Times,* December 1, 1968.

POP ICONOLOGY:
LOOKING AT THE COKE BOTTLE

by

Craig Gilborn

POP ICONOLOGY:
LOOKING AT THE COKE BOTTLE

by

Craig Gilborn

The redoubtable Samuel Johnson was citing a condition and not offering a choice when he wrote in the preface to his *Dictionary* (1755), "I am not yet so lost in lexicography as to forget that words are the daughters of earth, and that things are the sons of heaven." Dr. Johnson did not elaborate about the two realms of words and things, but he may have been acknowledging that words are not capable of translating all of those attributes of an object that are a-vailable to, and integrated by, the human senses. The cliché about a picture being worth a thousand words should be enlarged to include things: *Any thing is worth a thousand words.*

Knowledge of an object means that we have had some experience with it, either directly or on some previous occasion with an object that is similar or identical to it. In an earlier article in *Museum News* I tried to convey the complexity and cultivation of this non-verbal knowledge as it is revealed in the performances of such object-centered specialists as the museum curator, the primitive hunter, and the pre-industrial men and women whose daily tasks presupposed a vast body of informed, firsthand experience. Narrowing the scope of the earlier paper, I will pick up the discussion at the point in which recent educational theory and practice were said to be seeking to provide students with the kinds of first-hand experiences that challenge and motivate the scholar and scientist in their pursuit of knowledge.[1]

Objects are capable of yielding a considerable amount of information about themselves and the conditions in which they were formed or fashioned. Scholars and scientists in fields such as art history and criticism, archeology, paleontology, and the life and earth sciences use terms and methodologies appropriate to their respective problems of studying primary, non-verbal data. Without minimizing the differences that exist among these disciplines that take objects for their main source of evidence, it is worth asking whether the analysis of objects may not involve common modes of perception and organization; and, if so, whether this residuum may not be applied, although in a highly schematic form, in schools and museums where some sort of introductory exercise in the study and handling of objects is both desirable and proper.

The "classic" Coca-Cola bottle is admirably suited for such an exercise. The Coke bottle has been manufactured for more than fifty years, a long history by modern standards. The bottle has maintained a continuity of form during this period, but with discernible modifications from which relative and absolute chronologies can be obtained without resorting to any evidence but that presented by a sample of the bottles. Coke bottles are found in large quantities throughout the United States (and in most nations of the world); they are inexpensive, expendable, durable, and possess sculptural and optical qualities of great complexity. Accompanying the Coke bottle is an extensive lore consisting of anecdotes, personal associations, and

behavior traits (e.g., the "Coke break") that amount to a "folk" tradition that is truly national in scope. Hence, the bottle is, by any practical educational standard, a model vehicle for the performance of those operations which are basic to the systematic analysis of most objects.

A number of operations are involved in the study of objects.[2] Three broad operations, each capable of further sub-division, are identified in the sequence in which they are generally carried out: description, classification, and interpretation. The charts, pictures, and discussion that follow are based upon these operations as they apply to a study of the "classic" Coca-Cola bottle.

Several cautionary remarks are in order. First, the exercise as outlined below cannot provide all of the experiences that are part of the work that is performed in the field. For instance, description for the archaeologist frequently includes an entire site, not simply the objects uncovered in the site. Occasionally, however, archaeologists must work without a true archaeological context, as when artifacts or other material objects have been scattered by flooding streams or bulldozers. Second, different disciplines place different emphasis upon the operations. Art historians seldom work out classifications, partly because the differences seem so much greater than similarities (especially in the fine or creative arts) and partly because it is presumed that previous scholarship has established classifications that are still useful. Finally, this project is aimed at providing instructors with information and suggestions that can help them introduce students to the study of artifacts. The application of this material in the classroom is a matter best left to the instructor, but it is advisable that students be allowed considerable freedom rather than be constrained by undue emphasis on detail.

DESCRIPTIVE OPERATION

This operation, as applied to the Coke bottle, would ask the student or team of students to describe the "classic" bottle (identified in fig. 2 as the Type) in terms of its attributes of shape, symbol markings, structural details, material, color, and the like. There are two objectives to this operation. The methodological objectives (1) provide a written and iconic record which can be consulted on other occasions, and (2) involve the student—or the scholar-scientist—as a learner of every detail of the object to be studied. In this exercise the learning objective is to *develop an awareness of the diverse attributional character of objects.*

Believers of the efficacy of words may find the attempt

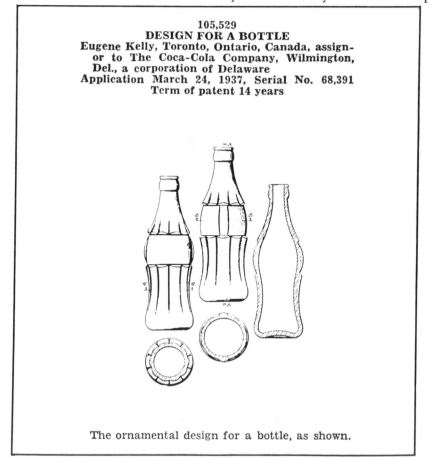

105,529
DESIGN FOR A BOTTLE
Eugene Kelly, Toronto, Ontario, Canada, assignor to The Coca-Cola Company, Wilmington, Del., a corporation of Delaware
Application March 24, 1937, Serial No. 68,391
Term of patent 14 years

The ornamental design for a bottle, as shown.

Fig. 1   Iconic Description

to describe the shape of the bottle to be a humbling experience. Metaphors have been used, but these are dated: "hobble-skirt," so called because of the design of the dresses worn when the classic bottle was introduced; "Mae West" and "hourglass." Hence line drawings are essential (fig. 1), and to these a nomenclature of visible attributes should be assigned. Some of these attributes will be generic in that they are expressive of the functional form that we call "bottle," involving the use of such terms as "mouth," "lip," "neck," and so on. There may be collectivities of attributes that indicate sections of the bottle, such as "top zone," "middle zone," or "front" and "back." Some attributes are peculiar to the Coca-Cola bottle itself, especifically the shape or design, the signatures "Coca-Cola" and "Coke" (all three trademarked), and the ribs. Some attributes, such as material, color, and weight, cannot be visualized iconically, though they must be a part of any proper description. Signs of wear should be noted if they occur. (In the bottlers' lexicon a "bum" is a bottle that can be safely re-filled, but that looks disreputable; a "scuffie" is a bum that is scuffed; and a "crock" is a bum with a chipped bottom.)

During this first operation, students may be given one bottle or one example from each of the three Sub-Types designated in figure 2. The latter choice will raise questions about differences that are to be dealt with in the classificatory operation.

CLASSIFICATORY OPERATION

The difference between description and classification is that the former treats each object as an entity—almost as if each were unique—whereas classification segregates objects on the basis of dis-similar attributes. An assumption at the outset of the classificatory operation is that there is an historical or functional relationship among the objects being classified, so that differences in attributes can be

		DIAGNOSTIC ATTRIBUTES	REMARKS
FAMILY		(1) "Coca-Cola" trademark and (2) Shape	6½, 10, 12, 16, 26 oz. returnables. Before 1957, beverage available only in 6 oz.. bottles.
TYPES		Above plus (1) "6" or "6½" fl. ozs. or (2) height 7¾ inches	Green glass in America, clear glass for foreign markets (except Japan)
VARIANTS	*Sub-Types*	Above plus All-B B&P, or All-P	
A 1915		Pronounced bulge	Prototype, designed by A. Samuelson, Terre Haute, Ind., U.S. patent No.48160. One surviving example illustrated in *The Coca-Cola Bottler*, June,1967 (pg.102).
B 1916-23		"Bottle Pat'd Nov. 1915"	Slimmed down to accomodate standard bottle filling equipment. Protected by first patent. Mold no., Mfr's mark and year appear either on heel or hobble.
C 1923-37		"Bottle Pat'd Dec.-25,1923"	U.S. design patent No. 63657.
D 1937-51	*All-Blown*	"Bottle Pat. D-105529"	Empty weight of bottle 14.01 oz., capacity 207.0 c.c. Bottle pat. March 24,1937. Year-Mfr's Mark-Mold Number confined (?) to hobble.
E 1951-59	6 ozs.	(1) "Min contents" "6-Fl. ozs" and (2) "In U.S. Patent Office"	Common law rights protection with expiration of patent. Mfr's Mark moved to base, leaving year-mold number on hobble, e.g. "53-21"
F 1957-65	6½ ozs	"6½ Fl. ozs."	Empty weight 13.80 oz, cap. 202.8 c.c. Second shape ever registered as a trademark (1960), protected while it identifies the product. Other trademarks: "Coca-Cola" (1893), "Coke" (1945).
G 1958-60	*Blown & Painted*	"Coke" not on throat	Transitional. Bottler's town ceases to appear on G,H, I.; re-appears on J. and K. Registration dimple appears. Empty Wt. 13.65 oz., Cap. 202.1 c.c.
H 1958-60		"Coke" on throat	Transitional. Painted labels appeared in 1956 but writer has seen none dated earlier than 1958.
I 1961-62	*All-Painted*	"Coke" on throat	
J 1963-65		(1) "Coke" on one panel & (2) "6½ oz" on one panel	Bottler's town re-appears on base of some bottles. Empty Wt. 13.26 oz., cap. 205.0 c.c.
K 1965-		"6½ oz" on both panels	Mfr's Marks: Ⓒ Chattanooga Glass Co.; Ⓘ Owens-Illinois; LG Liberty Glass Co.; L Laurens Glass Works; ⊥ Anchor Hocking.

Fig. 2. Classification

explained in terms of changed behavior or altered conditions, usually
as they have taken place over a
period of years.

There are two methodological
objectives to classification: first, as
suggested above, to reveal relationships that are real and not categorical
(for example, billiard balls and
tomatoes as "round, smooth" objects);
and, second, to provide a future reference against which freshly uncovered specimens may be compared and identified or otherwise
accounted for. The classification for the classic Coke bottle (fig.2)
serves both objectives by indicating relationships among the Sub-Types
and their Variants, and by providing a model for the identification of
bottles. Like most classifications, this one is subject to modification
or further refinement.

As for the learning objectives to this exercise, there are
three that should be mentioned. The first is that while all objects
consist of a variety of attributes, *some of these attributes are diagnostic
in that they identify groups or differentiate one group from another.*
Hence the attributes jointly diagnostic of the Family in figure 2 are
the Coca-Cola signature and the shape of the bottle. By contrast,
glass is not an attribute diagnostic of the Family, though it is descriptive in that it is an attribute common to all Coca-Cola bottles.

A second learning objective might show *the distinction
between relative chronology and absolute chronology.* It is possible
to arrange the three Sub-Types and/or Variants E through K in the
sequence in which they were introduced, using internal evidence and
the senses (including common sense) as means for proposing, for
example, that Blown & Painted (B&P) bottles fall between All-Blown
(A-B) and All-Painted (A-P) bottles. Deciding whether or not A-B
bottles came before A-P bottles might be answered in two ways. One
way is inconclusive, though it would probably lead to a correct choice
in the case of the Coke bottle: this would see the development of the
bottle proceeding from simple to more complex attributes, which

would suggest a relative chronology of A-B, B&P, A-P.

The second way involves the use of frequencies of occurrence, the principle being that earlier specimens will be those that are found in fewer numbers. Since all of the classic Coke bottles carry the date of manufacture, it is possible to establish the absolute chronology and the durations of Variants by examining a random sample of bottles and correlating date digits with the Variants. Sufficient numbers of Variants E through K survive to make this frequency analysis possible wherever Coke bottles are found; earlier Variants (A through D) must be identified largely through written and pictorial materials, such as, for example, U.S. patents (fig.1) and advertisements which illustrate these early Variants being used at times given by the date of publication.[3]

A third learning objective might *indicate the ways in which the systematic analyses of objects are capable of generating information or new knowledge.* The frequency approach, just cited, helps to verify what would otherwise be a highly theoretical classification the fact that Coke bottles can additionally be dated allows us to visualize the development of the Coke bottle and to raise questions about the possible human motivations or economic principles that lie behind the changes. For example, the sequence and durations of the manufacture of Variant bottles (fig. 3) indicates that while the

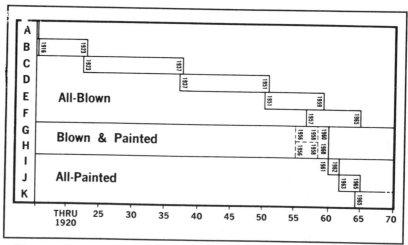

Fig. 3   Sequence and Durations (F-K based on frequencies)

Coca-Cola Company introduced
Variants one after another, there
was considerable overlapping in
the durations of manufacture, so
that during the years 1958-60 there
were four Variants being manufactured. These overlapping durations
notwithstanding, the "drift" from
blown to painted bottles is apparent
in figure 3. The implications of this
"drift" are presented in yet another chart (fig.4), which suggests that
some sort of evolutionary principle may have been operative in the
changes that have occurred in the Coke bottles of the last ten years
or so.

INTERPRETIVE OPERATION

Interpretation is the culminating objective since it
addresses itself to the broad question, *What possible meanings can
be derived from the products of our labors?*

For some scholars and scientists the objectives of description and classification constitute legitimate ends in their own
right. Classification, they might assert, is itself a form of interpretation,
though one that imposes conditions upon any attempt to depart
radically from recorded data. Others view interpretation as both an
opportunity and a responsibility for the informed imagination to
depart, if necessary, from facts to levels of generalization that may
not be entirely supported by the evidence at hand. Whether the
interpretation is modest or daring, a step or a leap from the known
to the unknown, will depend upon the nature of the problem and the
materials being dealt with, the criteria of truth accepted by the profession involved, and the personal abilities and inclinations of the
interpreter.

The following capsule analyses represent three (undefined)
levels of generalization.

*History.*Coca-Cola was invented and first sold in Atlanta,
Georgia, in 1886, by a pharmacist, John S. Pemberton.[4] Six years later the

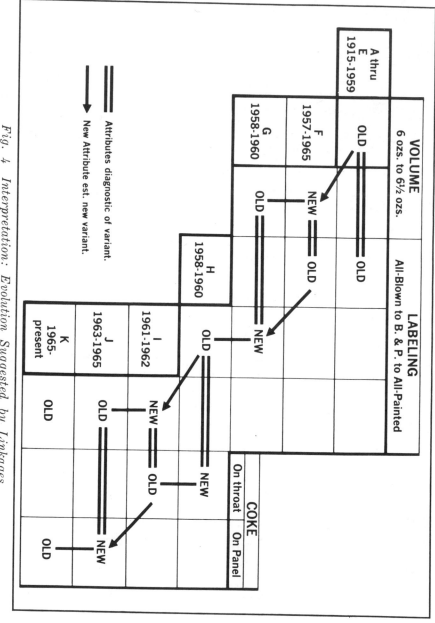

Fig. 4 Interpretation: Evolution Suggested by Linkages

business was incorporated as "The Coca-Cola Company;" a year later, "Coca-Cola" was registered in the United States Patent Office. The company adopted an aggressive policy aimed at winning public favor. By 1901 the advertising budget reached one hundred thousand dollars, a sum increased tenfold within the next ten years.

Coca-Cola was first bottled in 1894. Between that year and 1915 the beverage was sold in straight-sided bottles of varying colors and designs. To protect their product from imitators, the company adopted and patented a design devised in 1915 by Alexander Samuelson, an employee of the Root Glass Company, of Terre Haute, Indiana. Except for the slimming down of the initial design and changes in the labeling characteristics, the basic form of the "classic" bottle has remained essentially unaltered.

Presently there are three registered trademarks—"Coca-Cola" (since 1893), "Coke" (since 1945), and the design of the bottle (since 1960), the last being previously protected by a succession of design patents and common law rights. The bottle is manufactured by six glass companies in twenty-seven factories in the United States. Foreign bottlers obtain their bottles from manufacturers in countries of origin--and with labels in many languages. Nearly 6.6 billion Coke bottles were manufactured between 1916 and 1960 in the U.S. By 1966 the beverage was being sold in 132 countries and territories around the world.

Popular Culture. America's pop artist, flamboyant recorders of the commonplace, singled out the Coke bottle as one of their earliest subjects. The first "pop" depiction of the bottle was Robert Rauschenberg's "Coca-Cola Plan," a sculptural construction of 1958 incorporating three bottles. Among other early treatments was Andy Warhol's large canvas of 1962 illustrating 210 Coke bottles. The bottle's unparalleled success as a commercial and cultural symbol (Raymond Loewy called it the "most perfectly designed package today") is suggested by an egg and a

Coke bottle in a still-life painting done for the author by Jonathan Fairbanks.
The sacred and the profane are confounded by these juxtapositions,
in which the mysteries of art are appropriated by the clutter of everyday life.

The Coke bottle is the most widely recognized commercial
product in the world. Only one person out of four-hundred was unable
to identify a picture of the bottle in a product recognition study under-
taken in 1949.[6] The bottle is one of the few truly participatory objects
in the United States and in much of the world. Presidents drink Coca-Cola,
so do sharecroppers. Usage cuts across nationalities, social and occupationa
classes, age groups. The bottle, unlike most other objects which might
be regarded as symbols *par excellence* of American culture, is singularly
free of anxiety-producing associations. It is regarded with affection by
generations of Americans brought up in gasoline stations, boot camps,
and drug stores, and evokes pangs of nostalgia when Americans gather
in the cafes of Europe and Asia.

Evolutionary Change. Evolution in the biological world
has been applied to the civilizations and institutions of the human world.
The extra-Darwinian use of evolutionary thought has been largely
metaphorical--a means of visualizing the human story as a succession of
periods following one another according to some presumed necessary
developmental logic. Previous civilizations seem to have passed through
periods of youth, maturity, and decay; but is this due to the preconception
of historians or is it rather an expression of some profound law governing
the development of human societies? Institutions and their products
may provide evidence that can be more readily observed than the larger
society of which they are a part.

Taking the Coca-Cola bottle, we find that evolution of
a sort has taken place, beginning in 1955 when the company introduced
bottles that were partially painted. The older all-blown bottle, which
had seen service since 1916, remained in production while the company
determined the public's response to the greater visibility provided
the white label against the brown beverage. Between 1955 and 1965

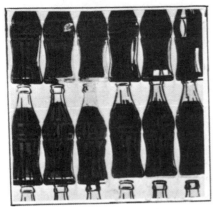

the company introduced six Variant bottles in succession, each Variant introducing a new attribute (fig.2). What is interesting—and perhaps significant—is the progression in which a new attribute in an earlier Variant became an old attribute in a later Variant, so that each Variant since 1955 has linked old-new attributes. The relationship is represented in figure 4.

Do these linked attributes indicate the operation of some evolutionary principle? One might say that each change in the Coke bottle is the result of some overall corporate plan, and that the underlying decisions are arbitrary. But corporate decisions are predicated upon the future success of the product in the marketplace. When the product cannot adapt to changing patterns of buying habits, it will fail or become obsolete—the artifactual equivalent of extinction in the natural world.

In the 1950s the Coca-Cola Company was not expanding its sales to the satisfaction of its directors.[7] Other beverage producers were responding to an affluent consumer market that was willing to buy new varieties of flavors in a range of sizes. The Coca-Cola Company met the competitive challenge by adding four sizes of bottles and the metal can to the established "classic' bottle. (The non-returnable bottles are yet another, more recent, development.)

The old workhorse bottle must have presented a problem: How could it be modified without damaging its demonstrated effectiveness as a seller of Coca-Cola? The answer was a gradual change of the bottle over a ten-year period, retaining the familiar all blown bottle down to 1965 and introducing between 1955 and 1965 a series of painted bottles whose modifications would become familiar and hence acceptable to the public. Raymond Loewy presented the dilemma facing corporate planners and industrial designers when he wrote that the "consumer is influenced in his choice of styling by two opposing factors: (a) attraction to the new and (b) resistance to the unfamiliar."[8]

That a degree of stability has been achieved after a decade of change is indicated by the fact that Variant K has been the only "classic" bottle in production since 1966 (fig. 3).

Other questions that invite   interpretation are:

What are the sensuous (touch, sight, etc.) and psychological qualities that contribute to the effectiveness of the Coke bottle?

How might archaeologists of a future millenium use the bottle in reconstructing the events and forces of the twentieth century?

What kinds of ritualized behavior accompanies the drinking of Coca-Cola from bottles?

Compare the changing historic roles of the Christian cross, the American flag, and the Coca-Cola sign in the non-Western nations of the world.

Several points might be noted in conclusion. While words are not a substitute for first-hand experience, they are the most efficient means of organizing and communicating a part of that experience to oneself and to others. Dr. Johnson's remark, quoted earlier, should be pondered in much the same spirit of humility with which it was written words and things *are* different, but this is not to say that we must therefore choose between a life of pure conception or of unmediated experiences, a proposition that seems to underlie much of the thinking of those who criticize, and with justice, the traditional emphasis or reliance in education upon responses that begin and end with words, seldom consulting the world of the senses as a point of departure.

The second and third points are related, and they are formulated as questions. Are there common modes of perceiving and organizing evidence in artifacts? The Coca-Cola bottle is exceptional only because it provides opportunities for carrying out so many of the procedures that are part of the analyses of such diverse things as pre-historic pottery, candlesticks, and domestic architecture. Finally, do museums, as repositories of things and of the skills and knowledge which make these things understandable, have a legitimate role to play by clarifying, both for themselves and others, how objects may be used to inform the mind, but without burdening it with information that will be useless or forgotten a few years hence?

NOTES

[1]"Words and Machines: The Denial of Experience," *Museum News*, 47 (September, 1968), 25-29.

[2]See, for example, Irving Rouse, "The Strategy of Culture History," in *Anthropology Today*, (University of Chicago, 1958), 57-76.

[3]See, for example, issues of the *Saturday Evening Post* for July 9, 1932 and August 28, 1937 (Variant C); and for July 30, 1938 and July 24,1943 (Variant D).

[4]The single most complete source of historical information is the fiftieth anniversary issue of *The Coca-Cola Bottler*, LI (April, 1959), 243 pp.

[5]"Portrait of a Product," *Art in America*, 52 (April, 1944), 94-5.

[6] E.J. Kahn, *The Big Drink* (New York: Random House, 1960), 155-56.

[7]Jack B. Weiner, *Dun's Review*, 88 (October, 1966) p.28ff.

[8]*Never Leave Well Enough Alone* (New York, 1951), 279. See, also, Robert W. Sarnoff, "Anatomy of the New Trademark," *Saturday Review*, 51 (April 13,1968), p. 91ff.

SELECTED READING

APPLICATION

Anon., "Analysis of the Buttons from the Ruins at Brunswick Town and Fort Fisher, N..C., 1726-1865." Typology, on sheet with legend "N.C.Dept. of Archives and History, South 10/63"

James Deetz and Edwin S. Dethlefsen, "Death's Head, Cherub, Urn and Willow," *Natural History*, 76 (March, 1967), 28-37.

Bernard L. Fontana, "The Tale of a Nail: On the Ethnological Interpretation of Historic Artifacts, *The Florida Anthropologist*, XVIII (1966), 85-90.

Ivor Noel Hume, *Treasure in the Thames*. London: Frederick Muller, 1956.

Henry C. Mercer, "The Dating of Old Houses," *Old Time New England, XIV* (April, 1924), 170-190.

Stanley J. Olsen and J. Duncan Campbell, "Uniform Buttons as Aids in the Interpretation of Military Sites," *Curator,* V (Nov. 4,1962), 346-352.

H. Stuart Page, "The Evolution of English Pottery: Suggestions for a Type-Collection," *The Museums Journal, 11 (*September, 1911), 61-76.

Raymond B. Wood-Jones, *Traditional Domestic Architecture of the Banbury Region.* Manchester: Manchester University, 1963.

THEORY

Roger Brown, *Words and Things.* Glencoe, Illinois: The Free Press, 1958.

V. Gordon Childe, *Piecing Together the Past: The Interpretation of Archaeological Data.* New York: Praeger, 1956.

David L. Clarke, *Analytical Archaeology.* London: Methuen & Co., 1968.

Henry Glassie, *Pattern in the Material Folk Culture of the Eastern United States.* Philadelphia: University of Pennsylvania, 1968.

George Kubler, *The Shape of Time: Remarks on the History of Things.* New Haven: Yale, 1962.

George Gaylord Simpson, *Principles of Animal Taxonomy.* New York: Columbia University, 1961.

William Duncan Strong, "Historical Approach in Anthropology," in *Anthropology Today,* (Chicago: University of Chicago, 1953), 386-398.

Hugh R. Walpole, *Semantics, The Nature of Words and Their Meanings.* New York: W.W. Norton, 1941.

SOFT DRINKS AND HARD ICONS

by

Arthur A. Berger

SOFT DRINKS AND HARD ICONS

by

Arthur A. Berger

It is possible, I think most people would agree, to make certain generalizations about national preferences as far as beverages are concerned. Thus, the French, Italians and Spaniards (Mediterranean peoples) are wine drinkers and coffee drinkers, the English, Germans, Dutch, Scandinavians and Americans (Atlantic Peoples) are beer drinkers, and, except for the British, coffee drinkers. The Americans and the British are great hard liquor (fermented grains) drinkers, whereas the Europeans tend to be brandy and cognac (fermented wine) drinkers, though hard liquor is making its way all over the world.

Two of the most important types of American beverages, however, are the ubiquitous *Coca-Cola,* which has spawned a whole genre of soft-drinks all over the world, and the malted milk. The latest refinements in soft-drinks are diet soft-drinks, which permit one to have the best of both worlds:[1] pleasure (quench thirst?) without consequences (getting fat).

        This catalogue, which is very general, is not meant to suggest that Americans don't drink a great deal of wine (they do) or tea (they are beginning to), but Americans are not wine drinkers or tea drinkers as a rule. The following chart presents the dynamics of drinking in a more understandable and obvious manner:

NATIONAL BEVERAGES

Country	Mild-Alcoholic Beverages	Meal or Dessert Beverages	Miscellaneous Beverages	"Hard" Liquor
America	Beer	Coffee	Coca-Cola Malted Milk	Whiskey
Great Britain	Beer	Tea	Derivative carbonated beverages	Whiskey
France	Wine	Coffee	Derivative carbonated beverages	Cognac Brandy
Italy	Wine	Coffee	Derivative carbonated beverages	Cognac Grappa

        We have not been particularly creative in terms of developing different kinds of alcoholic drinks, as the French or Italians have, for instance. They make drinks out of everything imaginable, from artichokes to flowers; where we have been inventive is in producing mass-consumption, mass-production, soft drinks of which

Coca-Cola is the best known example.

A cola is defined as a carbonated soft drink flavored with extracts from coca leaves, kola nut, sugar, carmel, plus acid and aromatic substances. A Coca-Cola generically is a distant cousin to cocaine—this relationship is obvious just in the makeup of the words. Cocaine is a narcotic and local anesthetic, and both of these qualities, I would say, suggest something about American life. To the extent that Coca-Colas are second-rate narcotics and anesthetics, they represent an attempt, which is unconscious, by Americans to move beyond reality, to escape it. Thus "The Pause That Refreshes" can be understood in several ways: on the most literal level it cools us off, it freshens us up (and, remember, freshens means *arouse* and *stimulate*); also, on another level, it allows us to escape from everyday life by moving into some kind of a dream world or by dulling our senses so that the real world doesn't impinge on us so greatly.

The appeals that Coca-Cola and Pepsi-Cola make stress youth, which points to the fact that these beverages are now being palmed off as elixirs--prolonging youth, changing base metals to gold (old age to adolescence) and renewing. Although both the colas present images of cleancut youth having "fun," it is well to remember that one of the meanings of refresh is to arouse. The cleancut, good-looking girls who drink the frosty colas are, at the same time, both escaping from the real world, its pains and inhibitions, and being aroused. In that sense, the colas are more involved than malted milkshakes, which represent a desire for the breast and the simplicity and serenity of infancy.

It has been pointed out that the Coca-Cola bottle does look like a breast and quite possibly functions as a breast substitute for many people. Psychologists have suggested that people think of soft-drinks as luxury items with which they can reward themselves. The size of the industry and the spread of Coca-Cola all over the world make it hard to offer generalizations about the significance of colas and American society, but there are several factors that must be considered. First, much Coca-Cola is consumed because it is one of the few safe things to drink in many countries. Secondly, it is very American, and for many people partaking of Coca-Cola involves being progressive, being "American." So despite its world-wide popularity Coca-Cola and its competitors are essentially American phenomena and have meaning and relevance as far as the American scene is concerned.

The latest phenonenon in the soft-drink industry involves "diet drinks," that is drinks with sugar-substitutes that cut down on the calories and yet provide all the "pleasure" that is desired. Diet drinks such as Tab, Diet-Pepsi, etc. work on the principle I call "The pleasure without consequences wish," and as such, are a triumph over some traditional American conceptions and are perhaps the hallmarks of a new society.

One of the great distortions in the American mind is that the Puritans were all sour and solemn. From them, according to popular belief (which is wrong) we discover that all pleasures have their consequences, that you cannot have pleasure without pain, and as it is thought, pain is a necessary part of life—perhaps even the most important part. According to this logic, whatever is pleasant is really bad for you and whatever is unpleasant (such as foul tasting medicine) is in reality good for you. Thus, the Puritans are supposed to to have told us, you cannot have your pleasure without consequences, so if you drink Coca-Colas you will get fat. With diet drinks, all of a sudden you learn that you can have your *pleasure without con-sequences!* You can guzzle soft drinks until you are bloated like a pig and not worry—since there are only five or six calories in every bottle of the diet drinks.

How this principle will affect the regular colas is hard to know. The two kinds of colas represent different principles: escapism versus pleasure, here and now, without consequences. I suspect that the major market for the diet drinks is calorie-conscious men and women, so that diet colas are not quite as significant as their parents, and despite their rocketing sales, are not so popular— yet. When you join the "Pepsi Generation," then, not only are you trying to escape your individual identity and merge into some kind of a group, but you are also trying to escape yourself and ultimately the world.

I might add, in closing, that Coca-Cola's rationale is a

typically conservative American one, so that we have the fitting
parallel of an American product mouthing an American "line." In
a little brochure entitled "Why" that explains Coke's popularity we
find that it is "pure as sunlight" (for the Puritan in us), natural—ingredients from nine countries but "no other flavoring agents are
added" (for the a-historical American) and relatively low in calories
(Coke has 12.1 calories per ounce versus 12.2 for other imitators).
But the main argument is a variation of Pope's "Whatever is, is right."
Coke says that its popularity "must be deserved" and "it had to be
good to get where it is." Its success becomes its justification. What
we have then is a perversion of Pragmatism which says, more or less,
that if something is good it will work, *not* if something works it is
good. With Coke's type of argument there is no room for change and
no justification for anything but "success." This emphasis on
achievement, regardless of the means used, is an American characteristic
which numerous sociologists have discussed in great detail.

Coca-Cola has just adopted a new advertising theme,
"Things Go Better With Coke," which suggests that it is somehow
instrumental in improving the world. Despite the fact that billions
of Cokes are consumed every week, things don't seem to be getting
any better. That, perhaps, is the answer. If you have enough Coke,
if you anesthetize yourself sufficiently, things seem to be better
than they are. Inevitably, of course, the soft drinks prove inadequate
and you move on to hard drinks ever trying to evade "the morning
after."

NOTE

[1]You can now have your "cake" and drink it, so to speak. The
recent discovery that cyclamates may cause cancer was a complicating factor,
but other sweetening agents have been found and the pleasure-without-pain
principle is still operating.

FURTHER THOUGHTS ON ICONS

by

Marshall McLuhan

FURTHER THOUGHTS ON ICONS*

by

Marshall McLuhan

Editors' note:
     Ever since his *Mechanical Bride* presented the lady herself as a sort of manufactured manipulated icon, Marshall McLuhan has explored and explained the iconic quality of contemporary life. Post-mechanical man is the Gadget Lover. Like the mythic Narcissus we have adapted to the echo which is an extension of ourselves, and thus become closed systems. Electric technology is a live model of the central nervous system itself. This, for McLuhan, posits a whole new set of popular icons.
     Some of them get individual chapters in his most influential book, *Understanding Media: The Extensions of Man*–Clock, car, type-writer, telephone, phonograph, radio, TV set. He recalls that on his

deathbed Henry James called for his Remington typewriter to be worked near his bedside. Were a later model not working this very minute, you, dear reader, would never be reading this page.

McLuhan has also written about the War of the Icons, which has long been under way. "Ink and photo are supplanting soldiery and tanks," he notes. 'The pen daily becomes mightier than the sword."[1]

Electric persuasion, he maintains, dunks entire populations in new images of popular icons. In addition to these new icons, there are always the old ones, seen in the rear view mirror as we speed forward. One of the most traumatic features of the painful switch from mechanica to electric technology is that it creates a myriad of icons. To live with both sets of technology and icons at the same time is the peculiar drama of the twentieth century. He recalls words which Shakespeare put into the mouth of his Julius Caesar:

> Between the acting of a dreadful thing,
> And the first motion, all the interim is
> Like a Phantasma, or a hideous Dream:
> The genius and the mortal instruments
> Are then in council; and the state of man,
> Like to a little Kingdom, suffers then
> The nature of an insurrection.

Dramatic things have happened in our little Kingdom even in the few years since McLuhan published *Understanding Media.* Man has left his planet, landed on the moon, and brought back rock samples to be placed beside other icons in museum cases. Through the lens of Astronauts' cameras we have all seen our earth from outer space—a cosmic baseball spinning in endless space. Plainly the globe has become a kind of art object. Is it also the ultimate icon?

Such thoughts prompted us to seek from Marshall McLuhan his current thoughts on icons. Here is his reply.

+ + + + + + + + + + + + + + + + + +

Since writing the earlier essay, my studies of the icon have developed considerably. As an audile-tactile form of resonant interface, it gets attention in *Through The Vanishing Point: Space in Poetry and Painting* (Harper & Row, N.Y. 1968) by Harley Parker and Marshall McLuhan.

The TV image is not so much pictorial as iconic because the TV tube projects figures rather than pictures. The TV camera has no shutter. Its "scanning finger" stresses outlines rather than light and shade. Especially since colour, the rear projection of the TV image has acquired much greater iconic force. That is one reason why non-white presences on TV are so much more effective than the white man's image. The white is weak on TV because of the light and shade or chiaroscuro effect which acts mainly on the periphery of the eye. Colour and bounding line or iconic contour, on the other hand, are received mainly by the *macula* or centre and cone area of the eye where the multitudinous interfaces of the cones create there the images of light and shade and movement which are apprehended by the outer areas of the eye.

It cannot be too much stressed that rear-projection, or "light *through*" rather than "light *on*," has a very much greater power to involve the viewer. The TV image is iconic, not only in its bounding line character, but in its dominant fact of flatness or two-dimensionality. In contrast, the movie camera with its lineal sequence of stills and its convergent lenses which stress angle and point of view, light on rather than light through, is at the furthest extreme from the TV image. The movie camera favours the private point of view, the detached spectator and the star system of private images. TV, on the other hand, demands corporate images and is highly unfavourable to the star system stress. The TV audience tends to become actor and participant rather than star-gazer.

The TV camera is a Cyclops, a one-eyed monster, which merges the *gestalt* of figure and ground and turns the viewer into a kind of hunter. Unlike the movie, TV does not favour escapism or dream life. It is an inner, existential trip. The TV viewer not only tends to suppress mentally the action of one of his eyes, but tends strongly to play the total field rather than to concentrate on any particular target. In this way, TV is not only consistent with the war on pollution, but one of the major contributing causes to our awareness of pollutants as environmental facts. I would also point out that just as the booze panic of the 20's came with the jazz age and the initial retribalizing of the West, so the drug panic of the 60's came with the inner trip that is the act of the TV viewer. In effect, the TV viewer is "stoned." He doesn't need chemical drugs in addition. In the same way, the radio fans of the 20's in the first onset of tribal togetherness had no need to booze to counteract the up-tight remoteness and inhibitions of the old Wasp culture.

"The War of the Icons" has many new dimensions in politics and in advertising. The phrase "Love Thy Label As Thyself" is now for real, around the world. The icon may be ethnic, verbal, chemical, or personal. It has created totally a new figure-ground pattern of resonant intervals and metamorphosis in the West. Modern quantum mechanics insists that the chemical bond is resonance. There are no connections in the material world, only auditory intensities. In a word, science has gone iconic also since Heisenberg and Bohr. To understand the interplay of the icons today is to have the key to every level of action and change.[2]

NOTES

[1] Marshall McLuhan, *Understanding Media: The Extensions of Man* (New York, McGraw Hill, 1964), p. 294.

[2] Apropos the different audience responses to front and rear projection, even with the movie alone, a properly conducted experiment was carried out at Fordham University in 1967 by Eric McLuhan. The results are reported in *Monday Morning* Magazine, May, published in Toronto, 1968.

POP ICONS

by

Nicolas Calas

POP ICONS

by

Nicolas Calas

Since modern art became the art of the Establishment,
its opponent has been anti-art. The dispute between the champions
of art and the sponsors of anti-art brings to mind the famed eighteenth-
century quarrel between the proponents of the art of the ancients,
in the name of perfection, and those of the moderns, in the name of
progress. Today modern art is viewed in terms of art history, and
anti-art in terms of 'life'.

During the 1920's, Surrealism was Cubism's anti-art,
as Pop Art is the anti-art of Expressionism. In the 1937 *Portrait of
a Lady,* Picasso reinterpreted Cubist multiple planes in psychological
terms, suggesting split personality by fusing the side and front view

of a face into one; the second eye is between two noses, or the two
eyes are shown frontally and the single nose in profile.[1] The distance
between his Cubist *Fernande* and his Surrealist Dora Maars might be
measured in terms of the distance between Apollinaire and André
Breton.

   During this, the seventh decade of our century, doctors
of philosophy would prefer to 'pre-empty' Pop Art of anti-art. Study
of paintings in terms of basic patterns zeroes the difference between
Roy Lichtenstein and Nicholas Krushenick; concentrically zeroes
that between Jasper Johns and Kenneth Noland; squares that between
Andy Warhol's bouquets and Josef Albers' rectangles. If form is the
basic criterion for judging art, then why not also compare a basic
pattern of two different paintings to analogous patterns found in
nature? Why not compare the dots of a Lichtenstein to the spots
of a ladybird, and Poons' dots to the dots of that other insect, known
to the uninitiated in entomological classifications as a false ladybird?
Don't let us *pointilliste* our eyes! The integration of anti-art into
art is undoubtedly a valid preoccupation, allowing the erection of
partitions. What would museums do without walls? If the critic's
role is to establish that anti-art is art, perhaps a sibyl will prophesy
the coming of anti-critics.

   Let us enjoy images as images, as we enjoy games for
the sake of playing. Addiction to images is a dream derivative. To
be communicated in visual terms, sights seen, whether in sleep or in
the world around us, must be given form in a selected medium.
Since a reproduction is not intended to be confused with its original,
the artist in his painting will include only those aspects of the beheld
which he either wishes to or is able to reproduce. Pictures of reality
or of dreams that have crucial cultural impact are icons. In our
century the first great icons are Cubist. Thus, in his post-Euclidian
vision, Picasso projected on a single plane a synthetic view of the
multiple planes of a man playing the violin.

   From the Book of Daniel and from our dreams, we have
learned that the key images are those of people and places. Portraits
and landscapes are the bread and wine of painting. Let them be
nourishing and appetizing, fermented and stimulating! The early

Cubist paintings are exquisite. The guitar, the bottle of wine, the *journal,* the stilled cinematic descent provide glimpses of those non-Dutch interiors where the sophisticated *bourgeois* speculated on Bergson, Apollinaire, and Jurès. The Cubist's dissection of form corresponds to the socialist's critique of institutions and to the psychologist's analysis of man. Cubism endowed us with a post-Ptolemaic 'Fayum' image of man (a preview of Byzantine icons), but not with a post-Copernican view of the world. The Industrial Revolution outspeeded clocks, but the Futurist's view of the phenomenon remained trivial, and was exploded by de Chirico in the name of anxiety. Moreover, with de Chirico's biscuits, matchboxes, and fish mould, anti-art elements were introduced into modern art. From his *Gare Montparnasse* back to Palladio, through a metaphysical reality, a world of false dreams is unravelled. Anxiety is indirectly derived from the Greek word *gonier* (corner). De Chirico, Ernst, Magritte, Tanguy are cornered. What relics are to worshippers of icons, Dada and Surrealist objects are to the devotees of modern icons, i.e., things that possess an element of magic, of having been made without hands, as Marcel Duchamp's term 'ready-made' implies; of having been assembled by a mysterious force—the Surrealist found object.

Difficulty of legibility is what Cubism and Surrealism have in common; Cubist statements are not clear; Surrealist meanings are obscure. Matisse and Léger are undoubtedly the twentieth century's great masters of clarity, and their influence today on both Pop and abstract artists is indisputable. Their ability to simplify is admirable, but I object to the casual manner in which they treat their subject matter. Are Matisse's odalisques pure imitations of Persian women, or are they *Vogue* imitations of French women? Are Léger's workers militant members of the proletariat or performers of a *ballet mécanique?* This weakness of Matisse becomes glaring when we look at Wesselmann's *Great American Nudes*—prototypes of America seen through the mass media. The weakness of Léger becomes obvious when the paintings are re-examined through the middle-class character of Leger's proletarianism. Pop artists, by forgetting even the immediate past, focus their attention on the 'positivism' of the present.

After the fermented light of the Impressionists, the
aromatic pines and apples of Cézanne, the intoxicating colours of
the Fauves, the alcohol of dreams of the Surrealists, defeated Paris
was reduced to the imageless insomnia of Existentialism. The centre
of art moved to New York. With the self-assurance of Periclean
Athens, New York mixed its Doric and Ionic elements. American
Abstract Expressionism detached automatism from the Surrealist'
imagistic painting and, in so doing, liberated abstract art from its
obsession with geometric form. Now we can make and appreciate
the distinction between automatic abstraction and calculated abstraction
Historically, abstract art has its roots in Protestant and Judaic iconoclasm. It should be born in mind that France is the only great power
in Europe which, due to the atheist spirit of the Revolution of 1789,
passed from the medieval Catholic religion to the modern world
without going through the iconoclastic phase of Protestantism. In
France all the great movements of modern art, from Impressionism
to Surrealism, experimented with images. Max Ernst, the most important German Surrealist painter, comes from a Catholic family. In
England and in the United States, two countries with a Protestant
culture, the current battle for the image is waged on behalf of a
previously scorned image, the popular advertisement of consumer
goods. The lowly ad is easily viewed as anti-art. An orthodox Surrealist sees no virtue in its use since the ad lacks reference to the
esoteric. Surrealism opposes the dream to daydreaming and the myth
to reality. Furthermore, emphasis on consumer goods is offensive to
the Surrealist on ideological grounds, for he rates production over
consumption. Iconoclasm explains why many abstract artists are
more shocked by Pop artists' profanation of images than angered by
their rejection of abstract art.

Lichtenstein, Wesselmann, and Warhol are no more Pop
artists in the original British sense of the term than were Duchamp or
Léger Futurists in the Italian sense. If the Italian Futurists had a
Vulcan complex, the British Pop artists can be said to have a cornucopia
complex, that is to say, a love-hate attitude toward America's wealth
as they envisage it through the glossy American magazine.[2]   In New
York, ready-made vernacular images were first convincingly introduced
into works of art by two former Abstract Expressionists, Larry Rivers

and Robert Rauschenberg. Followed by Jasper Johns, Jim Dine, and Claes Oldenburg, these artists disfigure the ready-made image to adapt it to an over-all indeterminate pattern. Lichtenstein, Wesselmann, Warhol, and D'Arcangelo interpret the ready-made image in terms of calculated abstraction. With the former, the process of making is frequently interrupted by accidents, and with the later, the formation of images conforms to a definite pattern.

In terms of significance these tendencies are complementary. We would be like the naive Pre-Raphaelites looking at Botticelli without remembering Piero della Francesca if we included in our collection of icons Lichtenstein but not Rauschenberg, Rosenquist but not Rivers, Wesselmann but not Katz. But D'Arcangelo belongs and Fairfield Porter does not. By this I do not mean that the aesthetic contradictions of our time have to be resolved in terms of the humanist's concepts of beauty and truth. The contemporary imagists are searching for ways of assimilating a pictorial experience embracing the miniature comic-strips and the giant billboards. The illustrated weeklies demonstrate that the reproduction of *The Syndics* by Rembrandt can double as the trademark of Dutch Masters cigars. Why not also include a third version—Larry Rivers' painting of the Dutch Masters ad? Is a ruined Greek temple a historical monument or a TWA ad? What if it turned out to be a Lichtenstein?

Reproduction of the masterpiece refers to an object that is priceless because it is evaluated in historical terms, while the advertisement employing the historical piece refers to a commodity—a pack of cigars or an aeroplane ticket. Unlike the reproduction of the masterpiece that is meant to evoke the past, the ad encourages us to forget the past by inviting us to satisfy transient urges, to smoke or to travel; the picture of a 1966 Chevy makes us forget the 1965 Chevy; the beauteous Miss Rheingold distracts us from the home where beer is drunk without her. Surrealism sought to overcome the contradiction between desire and reality on the plane of a super-reality. Pop Art deals with a reality that is apt to be the printed reproduction of an image. However, the identification of the reproduction with its model is blocked when we realize (with the help of a magnifying glass) that the image dissolves into the pattern of the grid formed by the Ben Day dots. The grid's network is the threshold on which the reproduction and the printing process meet on an anti-image level. When Lichtenstein focuses on this threshold he forcefully dissociates his blown-up view from the comic-book universe. Jasper Johns achieved similar effects in the mid-1950's when he fused the design of the Star-Spangled Banner with the brushstroke patterns of the encaustic surface. Pop Art can be anti-Pop. Dissociations permit one to dismiss and, eventually, to forget the original. In their time, Surrealists such as Magritte, Tanguy and Ernst reawakened buried instances of a personal past and evoked that which is most difficult to remember; the dream, wherein the past is represented under a disguise or mask. But Lichtenstein and Johns chose to veil appearances more lightly by simple technique—grid or encaustic— which add an element of the unexpected without hiding identity. While the Surrealists' effects presented enigmas and masked faces, the effects of the younger men can be best likened to the recognition of a face despite unaccustomed sunglass—as in Alex Katz's *Ada with Glasses.* With Rauschenberg, Rivers and their kin, the procedure varies in that they resort to disfiguring the image with brushstokes and drippings. Either method aims ultimately at personalizing the image.

      Lichtenstein has been criticized for his false madonnas. Similar objections could be raised against Wesselmann for degrading the nude, D'Arcangelo for counterfeiting the road to Bethlehem, Rosenquist for crashing sacrifices on the road[3], and Warhol for his hot-selling sepulchral flowers. Art is not a tranquillizer. 'Pop Art looks out into the world', says Lichtenstein. The Pop artists look out on the world through reproductions. They paint it the way the Surrealists painted the dream—photographically. Having rejected the role of spiritual sons to some great master, both the Surrealists and the Pop artists have been viewed as anti-artists. The major difference lies in their attitude. Whereas the Surrealist's is lyrical, that of the Pop artist is cool. Therefore the reaction to the Pop image should be cool. Whether that image is or is not a work of art is a secondary consideration. Does the worshipper of an icon of his patron saint care whether the representation is a masterpiece? The icon is for use, when warm for prayer, when cool for companionship. The same applies to the Pop artist's relics: the dead as lead flashlights of Jasper Johns, and the hand-made metal chocolates or hot dogs of Robert Watts, subtracted from the superficial world of imitation, occupy a place in a reality from which identity has been excluded. Robert Morris' *Swift Night Ruler* stirs our sensibility through our inability to distinguish the correct measure from the false; Aaron Kuriloff's fuse boxes are set in the twilight zone between function and uselessness. Pop Art discovered the Surrealism of the understatement.

ICON ON WHEELS:
SUPERICON OF POPULAR CULTURE

by

B. A. Botkin

ICON ON WHEELS:
SUPERICON OF POPULAR CULTURE

by

B. A. Botkin

Why is the automobile a supericon and what is the difference
between a supericon and a simple icon? In Marshall W. Fishwick's
definition, an icon is "an uncritically venerated object or person"
and "a tangible symbol of intangible meanings." But in contrast to
the ordinary symbol as a static "designator," S. Giedion makes a case
for the "potent symbol" as a dynamic "potent agent." In the golden
age of the symbol, which he sees as prehistory, the "potent symbol,"
writes Giedion, was believed "to possess the power of working magic
and thus of directly affecting the course of events: the wish, the
prayer, or the spell to be fulfilled."[1] In the sense of working quasi-
magic and performing miracles I conceive of the automobile by analogy

as a potent icon or supericon.

More than an idol or emblem, the supericon in its miracle-working potency resembles the fetish (an object superstitiously venerated for its magic power) and the totem (an animal, plant, or object religiously venerated as a symbol of a group and so as its protector and benefactor). As a fulfillment of man's universal dream of conquering time and distance and of the American dream of the open road as the road to freedom of activity and movement, to opportunity and success, and related goals in the American credo, the automobile is a supericon of popular culture. This is the culture of innovation and change, mass-produced, mass-distributed, and mass-consumed like the automobile itself, from which popular culture has absorbed some of the basic principles of presentation and exploitation in the mass organization of behavior, thought, and taste.

The importance of language as an instrument of suggestion and persuasion in winning acceptance for new inventions and other social and cultural innovations is in need of more study in popular culture, especially humor, inasmuch as innovation and novelty, fads and cults are basic to this culture. Primarily the appeal of the linguistic innovations and inventions of slang and wisecracks (which latter utilize and resemble slang in their desire to be expressive) is the appeal of inventiveness. But by a process of repetition and imitation the new and strange is more easily accepted when cloaked in the familiar and old, and, to avoid boredom, vice versa. Hence the use of parody, burlesque, and simply playing variations on a theme, so that old jokes are constantly being switched and new jokes switched back, to balance the inventive and the retentive. Throughout this process of change and exchange, by variation and adaptation—a process also familiar in folk transmission but more liable and susceptible to manipulation and exploitation in popular than in folk art—the theme or motif serves as formula, cliché, and stereotype to standardize the product, as it were, by a kind of assembly line process after Ford's example.

Thus in a collection of 1,564 Lizzie labels, including variants, made at the University of Oklahoma in 1929-31 (drawing on the entries in a Lizzie label contest conducted by the Criterion Theater in Oklahoma City during the showing of the film, *So This Is College*) and published as "An Anthology of Lizzie Labels" in *American Speech,* October, 1931, also in a previous article, *The Lore of the Lizzie Label,* in the same journal for December, 1930, many variants have been included to show the range of possibilities.

The sources and types of Lizzie labels are as various as their form. In the later of the above-mentioned articles the labels are classified under the following heads with examples as follows:

I. BORROWINGS
   1. *Quotations*
      Abandon hope, all ye who enter in.
      True love never runs smooth.
   2. *Familiar Sayings* (Popular, Colloquial, Proverbial, and Epigrammatic)
      Answer to a maiden's prayer.
      Why girls leave home.
   3. *Song, Play, and Movie Titles and Lines*
      I Ain't Got No Body. [On stripdown.]
      Runnin' Wild.
   4. *Advertising Slogans*
      Eventually, why not now?
      Prince Albert comes in a can.
   5. *Signs, Slogans, Labels, Mottoes, and Notices*
      Fads come and go, style endures.
      Not responsible for flying parts.
II. ADAPTATIONS
   Opportunity is still knocking.
   Plenty of pickup! I'll say.
III. INVENTIONS
   1. *Wisecracks*
      Just because I'm a rattler, don't think I'm a snake.
      The only time we pass a car is when it is going the other way.

2   *Rhymes*

    A. Collegiate
        We take nobody's smotherin' dust.
        To Oklahoma College for Women or bust!

    B. Ford Jokes
        When all other cars have gone dead,
        This one just chugs right ahead.

    C. Girls
        Flapper's delight—
        Open all night.

    In spite of changing styles in popular humor as in language and dress, and car design and gadgetry, the problems of the motorist as lampooned in the automobile epigrams of the first decade of the century and again in the Lizzie labels and wisecracks of the Twenties and the Thirties remain much the same, if a little worse.

    Here, first, is Richard B. Glaenzer in *The Century* for July, 1905 (p. 480):

AUTOMOBILIA OF PUNBAD THE RAILER

Judge not an auto by its smell: *all* comparisons are odorous.
A tack in the tire is as a thorn in the flesh: both are tiresome.
It is a short ride that hath no mending.
All does not go that glitters.
An auto is not without odor save in its own front seat.
Say not: "We shall return at five"; ye may return at sixes
    and sevens.
Oils well that ends well.
Approach railroads warily, lest they lead thee to heaven.
Though thou swear *by* thine auto seven times, the eighth
    time thou will swear *at* it: that is Kismet.
The horse goeth not ten parasangs an hour, neither doth he
    explode.
To speed is human; to be caught is—fine!

A collection of popular proverbial phrases and sayings and other floating material made among my students in 1933-34 yielded similar wisecracks on the perennial themes of reckless drivers, speed demons, road hogs, women drivers, back-seat drivers, etc.

The way some people drive you'd think they were going
     to a fire.
A car's just an accident looking for a place to happen.
Most reckless driving is done from the back seat.
A reckless driver and Hell are boon companions.
Last words of John Smith: Watch me beat that train to
     the crossing.
Just because you see the tracks is no sign the train has passed.
The way some people drive you'd think they owned the car.
The way some people drive you'd think they own the road
     when they don't even own the car.
The way some people steer a car, you'd think they was
     raised on a farm.
She must be an old teacher of mine, she won't let me pass.
Better to be 20 minutes late than 20 years early in hell.
A woman motorist wants only half the road but she wants
     her half in the middle.
Try our locomotives, they hit but once.
Slower, please, there's other fools driving.
Gasoline and alcohol don't mix.
Give her the gas, hell is only half full.
When you pass a car on the left, it's right; but if you pass
     on the right, it's wrong.

My interest in floating literature, in the form of image, symbol, and comparison, slang and wisecrack, was my entrée to car culture and thence to popular culture. This interest proceeded from my discovery in Oklahoma of the "oral, linguistic, and story-telling. . .aspects of folklore" as found among both students and oldtimers. Pursuing my folklore collecting and editing, I coined the word "Folk-Say" in 1928 as the title of a regional miscellany, four annual volumes of which I edited from 1929 to 1932.[2] The broad meaning of the word as it became a common noun minus the hyphen and as I later defined it is "what people have to say about and for themselves in their own way and their own words." Gradually it became differentiated in two directions: (1) "own stories," "as told by" accounts, literature by and about the folk and (2) "informal verbal expressions, such as proverbs and exclamations, among a relatively unsophisticated group of people" *(The American College Dictionary,* 1947).

Although Lizzie labels and wisecracks are more "popular" or "mass" than "folk" and so relatively sophisticated in taste and style, the word "folksay" could be stretched to fit them under the head of "subliterature" and "floating literature" —terms used by Albert Guérard in *Literature and Society* (1935). My own term for expressive language of this type was "floating linguistic material," which I saw as belonging alike to the literature of entertainment, information, and promotion, as embodied in automobile jokes and car names and slogans.

The predilection of floating linguistic material for the brief forms of song, story, and humor has a relation to the automobile as a carrier and accelerator of popular culture in that the speeding up of modern life creates a taste for short, snappy sayings, such as Lizzie labels and other wisecracks.

According to a University of Oklahoma alumnus folklorist, Acel Garland,

> We no longer care to follow a tale or a ballad
> through a long maze of development. We crave
> short anecdotes, witty songs, that are immensely
> incredible. In short, we have become inoculated
> with the spirit of the traveling man joke. . . .
> Where does this modern lore originate? At small
> house-parties, on long automobile rides into the
> country when boys and girls are piled into any kind
> of old car. There appears to be need for some kind
> of conversation to break the monotony of such
> intensive necking; so the youths recall their traveling

salesmen and the girls, not to be outdone, slyly
remember their *Whiz Bang*. . . .

 The question arises as to whether or not the
obscene stories and the *risqué* songs of a generation
should be included in its folklore. Certainly the
source of this type of lore is more purely 'folk'
than that of any other. 3

 A good deal of this floating literature became "paper literature"
when "written on whatever kind of paper is handy at the time of its
acquisition and surreptitiously memorized and distributed among
themselves by laborers, high-school students, and college undergraduates."
 One of the chief sources of this "paper literature" and one
of the most popular and best of the folksy humor magazines of the
Twenties was *Capt. Billy's Whiz Bang*, a magazine of "Farmyard Fun
and Filosophy" and "Pedigreed Bunk," edited and published by
W.H. Fawcett of Robbinsdale, Minnesota. The following automobile
jokes from its pages are of the same brew as the Lizzie labels and
wisecracks already quoted. These have to do with new slang created
by the automobile and with the Tin Lizzie.

                    Non-Skids?

   Two sheiks speaking.
   "I've gone three thousand miles without a puncture."
   "G'wan, I saw you at a dance the other night with
      a flat tire." —May, 1924, p. 42

   One of our local citizens was arrested the other day
   charged with stealing a front tire from a flivver. His
   defense was that he just casually picked the thing up,
   thinking it was a rubber band. —July, 1924, p. 10

[In 1925 *Whiz Bang*, emulating *Judge* and its Lizzie Label
contest, offered prizes for "signs for puddle-jumping Lizzies," e.g.
"Good-Bye, I'll run across you some day."–March, 1925, p. 29]

> A Rockville girl, who has walked home quite often
> this season from Crystal Lake after going there on
> automobile parties, was given a road map last week
> by her parents when she observed her 19th birthday.
> —December, 1925, p. 59.

The barnyard school of humor introduces a rustic note which is one of the paradoxes of the automobile's and the highway's breaking down of the separation between city and country. While the most obvious effect is the change in the way of life of rural and small town America, somewhat less obvious is the effect on the urban motorist and the motorized and urbanized generations. No sooner had the motorist learned to speed up and at the same time control his car than he learned to slow down in order to control himself and enjoy the countryside, with the result that he ultimately took to shunpiking to recover a degree of leisure and privacy. One of the side effects was the nostalgic revival of old customs and old times, the most conspicuous example being that of Henry Ford with his Dearborn museum, Wayside Inn, and country dance movement assisted by Mr. and Mrs. Benjamin B. Lovett.

In relation to old-time leisure and sociability the filling station and the garage partially replaced the blacksmith shop and the livery stable as loafing and gossip places. During the Twenties Dick Wick Hall, a Wickenburg newspaperman, created a sophisticated version of the cracker-box philosopher in a mimeographed newspaper which he published for distribution to his customers at his "Laughing Gas" station on Highway 60 at the town of Salome, Arizona ("Where She Danced!"). The *Salome Sun* was one of the unique fantasies of the motor age, combining advertising with humorous verse often printed as prose in Walt Mason style.

The following rhymes suggest Lizzie label themes, with additions

> In the good old days when we used to shake and shiver,
> the doctors recommended horseback riding for the
> liver; but nowadays they tell us: "Go get yourself
> a flivver and take the trip from Phoenix to the
> Colorado River."

Here's Luck to the Lady that Rides the Back Seat—
which takes muscle. She stands on her head & sits on
her feet—or her bustle. She has wished every day
that she had never left HOME. My, how she rants!
But now she feels gay, she has got to Salome—
"Where She Danced."

Hy didle diddle, this road is a riddle, where Cadillacs
stick in the sand and little Fords run when others
are done and ask for a helping hand. A good boost
like that ought to be worth at least 85¢, Henry, or
a new engine.[4]

    In revolutionizing transportation, as we have seen, the auto-
mobile has also influenced communication by transmitting ideas and
customs in addition to carrying people and goods and by exposing
and accelerating the exposure of Americans to both new and old ideas
and customs. In both material and intellectual culture the motorist
has become a "culture consumer," in Alvin Toffler's term, to a
greater degree and in greater variety than before culture became
motorized by the individually driven internal combustion engine.
Here the role of the automobile as a supericon is strengthened by
the fact that it has not only increased the opportunities for self-culture
and popular culture through travel but has also become a mixer of
cultures and sub-cultures—local, regional, national, and international,
rural, urban, folk, and popular—and an enricher through innovations,
including those of affiliated industries and social inventions.
    As a result of greater mobility and leisure and higher standards
of living there has been a multiplication and diversification of play
contacts, cravings, stimuli, and outlets as part of the change from a
work morality, in which play is a reward for or an interval in work,
to a fun morality, in which play becomes a commodity. A further
result has been the blurring or breaking down of the distinction between
work and play, with play invading business or replaced by hobbies,
which are neither work nor play. To this confusion the automobile
has contributed by adding pleasure to necessity and utility and

stimulating the play elements of ritual and fantasy in the use and enjoyment of the automobile. In car culture the play factor has also manifested itself in what Henry Ford would call the predominance of the emphasis on "pleasure" and "luxury" over "necessity," "simplicity," and "economy." Confer his famous announcement of the Model T in 1909: "Any customer can have a car painted any color that he wants so long as it is black." The answer to Ford's pronouncement was made in Lizzie labels and wisecracks satirizing the cheapness and homeliness of the Model T exaggerated to the point of burlesque in the dilapidated, superannuated collegiate flivver and jalopy.

In the field of play and pleasure the automobile has not only reflected but also affected changes in fashions, manners and customs, morals, thought, and taste. Nowhere has this interchange been more active than in the etiquette of love and courtship (especially as illustrated by the Lizzie label and other Ford jokes) in which the new sexual freedom of the Jazz Age found a ready ally and an easy outlet in the shared intimacy and escapism of the car. The liberties and excesses which were considered daring in the Twenties are more or less taken for granted today. Comparing the necking and petting of yesterday with today's smooching and "going steady," an informant explains: "I think that the trouble today is the car. They can park it, and they are alone in their little car—just two people alone in their own little car—and that's when things begin to happen. . . . Today, when they go, they go in cars. They don't see anything. They just neck in cars. And with that little roof over their head, there's nothing. There's no poetry in a car. That's why I think that love was much healthier and more beautiful in those days."[5]

One of the revolutions in American leisure brought about by the automobile was the change in the attitude toward travel. Formerly, as Bellamy Partridge points out, "there had to be an excuse for travel . . .family weddings and funerals. . .a honeymoon. . .the World's Fair. . .[a] centennial. . . . There no longer had to be any excuse. Every motorist began to travel just for the pleasure of riding around and seeing new places. . . . The urge to go places seems to have been a constituent part of the ownership of a motor car."[6]

For a long time driving about town or in the country with no

specific destination in mind was the favorite form of driving for
pleasure. This included the family Sunday drive, which satisfied
the desire to be seen as much as the desire to see. It was a continuation
of the rural horse-and-buggy age pastime of riding out to see how
one's neighbors' farms were looking or of the city Sunday drive in
the open carriage, to show off one's finery as well as one's turnout.
The teenager who cruises around town in a convertible, with the car
or transistor radio blaring forth a rock-'n-roll tune, or who drives to
the community lovers' lane or "passion pit" with his girl (following
the pattern of the young swain who rented a shiny buggy from the
livery stable to spark his sweetheart), or who joins his pals for joy-
riding or a pickup, is also driving for pleasure. The term is broad
enough to include all free-time driving for social, recreational and
touring purposes.

Whereas recreational driving once consisted in driving for the
pleasures of locomotion and local self-display and sightseeing or in
primitive experiments in cross-country touring, today the car not
only is fun but takes us to where the fun is, so that what was at first
a plaything has become a play necessity. At the end of the not-so-
open road is a neighborhood movie or bowling alley, a country club
or a baseball park, a hunting, fishing, camping, scenic or historic site,
a beach or a ski resort, a place in the country or a visit to the city,
for an afternoon or an evening, for a weekend or a vacation.

The mass leisure-time use of the car, like mass entertainment,
has created problems and responsibilities for layman and expert alike.
While the car has taught Americans to know America, from small
town and metropolis to wilderness, and to distinguish between superficial and meaningful sightseeing and landscape viewing, it has littered
and defaced the countryside, crowded the open spaces, and substituted
the tyranny of the car and the road for the tyranny of the home and
the home-town. While increased mobility has resulted in greater face-
to-face contact and communication among Americans, it has also
resulted in "nomadness" and "automania," with their cults of speed
and gadgetry. While the car has brought about a return to nature
and the simple life with a revival of camping, outdoor recreation, and
wilderness sports, it has produced an increased emphasis on luxury and

display in equipment and accommodations and has made a Coney Island out of the Great American Roadside.

Or with so much to choose from there is a return to the old purposelessness or indecision. "I thought of taking a trip," said my neighbor across the street. "Going anywhere in particular?" I asked. "No, just get in the car and keep going until I feel like turning back."

Like every modern sport, driving has given rise to fads, cults, and symbols surrounding the cultivation and exploitation of gadgetry and accouterments. It was not long before the automobile "drug on the market," in Waldo Frank's term for the narcotic effect of the car—the delusion of perpetual "self-motion," "idealized into the delusion of 'progress' "[7]—developed symptoms of automania and automobilism.

As defined by a Nassau County, Long Island, judge, automania is "an overobsession with the automobile as a status symbol, as a means of getting someplace in a hurry, as a vehicle for a flight from tensions, or to indulge in a craving to show off."[8]

In the next stage, automobilism carries the car craze from obsession to cult. This is the stage described by Robert H. Boyle as "a quasi religion, what with its concept of the car as power, its special set of doctrines and the extraordinary behavior patterns exhibited by its devotees. It embraces a number of cults given over to the veneration of a particular type of vehicle. There are cults devoted to the sports car, the classic car. . .the Indianapolis racer, the motorcycle. . .the kart. . .and, of course, the hot rod."[9]

Within the cult of the particular type of vehicle, there are also the cults of the personality of the individual car and of the personality of the owner. Between the two "way-out" cults—the foreign sports car and the hot rod cults—there are striking contrasts in decoration and costume. Each has its *mystique*, fetishes, and gambits.

The sports car is a special kind of exurbanite status symbol which has its roots in the leisure-class exclusiveness of the wealthy who were the chief consumers of the first and expensive automobiles. Yet the sports car aficionado prides himself not so much on his elegance as on his amateur standing in the "wacky world of motor sport." Besides professionalism the chief butts of his snobbery, according to Ken Purdy, are Detroit cars and "Disrespect for the

Machinery."[10] Like other automobile cultists the sports car enthusiast
has his special costume (down to pierced-back chamois driving gloves),
which is part of his image.

Later the black-leather jacket of the demon motorcyclist, sans
cap and goggles, became the uniform of the demon hot rodder. With
the organization of hot rodder clubs, club jacket and insignia were
added, the jacket being commonly of blue wool. The ultimate in
the "way out" is seen in the hot rodder's "Weirdo shirt" originated
and produced by Ed Roth, of Los Angeles. The design is air-brushed
on the shirt in fluorescent colors.[11]

The special paint job is another car status symbol which harks
back to the motorist's desire to give individuality and personality to
the car. Harold D. Leslie recalls with affection his first car, a 1914
Model T Ford which he bought in 1919 with his army discharge pay
of $125. But "The crowning achievement of my early motoring
career came when I broke with the rigid Ford tradition of black bodies.
With a few gallons of sea-green paint, I transformed the complexion
of my car from a somber black to a startling green, in keeping with
the burgeoning spring verdure just then coming out of long hibernation.
From that day on, my snappy turnout was known as the Green
Dragon."[12]

The hot rodder's totems, charms, fetishes include bongo drums
on the rear shelf, following the beatnik trend, and stuffed lions.
According to Lieut. Ron Root of Pomona, a member of the Police
Advisory Council for Car Clubs in Los Angeles County, as quoted
by Boyle, the stuffed lion "was the answer to our making them take
graduation tassels and baby shoes off the rear-view mirror. . . . One
of the things the kids do. . .is to take a cocktail glass, fill it with
acetate glue, put a red marble in it for a cherry or a green one for
an olive, and glue the base of the glass to the dashboard and let her
sit. Looks strange."[13]

As the hot rodder's idolatry of the car's "expanded body image"
is part of the anti-social revolution of automobilism, which reaches its
peak in the hedonism and anomie of the beat revolution (as seen in
Jack Kerouac's On the Road, 1955), so a counter-revolution (this time
against the car itself) has set in with the consumer's revolution (as seen

in John Keats's *The Insolent Chariots,* 1958, and Ralph Nader's *Unsafe at Any Speed,* 1965).

The present attack on the automobile as a major polluter and destroyer of the environment, natural and man-made, finds the ecologist teamed up with the urbanologists and planners, who were among the car's earliest critics, and the lawyers ("Nader's Raiders") among the latest. The case for and against the car is summed up by Jerry M. Flint in an article in the *New York Times,* entitled "The Car: Devil with a Halo," in a special supplement on the "International Automobile Show 1970," Section 11, Sunday, April 5, 1970. In his opening sentence the author straightens the devil's halo: "Like the army that loses all its battles but the last, the automobile society appears destined to last indefinitely." Then he continues: "The car stands before the bar of society convicted:

Of polluting the air with fumes and noise.
Of filling the streets with traffic jams and junked cars.
Of destroying the beauty of neighborhoods with gasoline
     stations and garages.
Of taking billions of dollars from consumers' pockets
     to correct shoddy engineering or workmanship.
Of killing nearly 60,000 persons a year.
And some feel its greatest guilt is that it has helped
     create urban sprawl and the destruction of the
     cities, allowing the more affluent members of
     society to escape the problems, leaving the blacks
     and the poor helpless in decaying cities."

Is the love affair with the automobile over?

Will the "lovers in automobiles" be the only "Automobile lovers"?– to borrow a pun from William Saroyan's *Short Drive, Sweet Chariot.*

Will ecology win the battle against technology?

While the automobile may be in trouble, serious trouble, it is still what Henry Ford called, when he saw the first automobiles on the street, "a necessity." And it may yet be made a safe and sane necessity if the technologists heed the ecologists and the urbanologists. Then the supericon, which, in the mythology of the machine and motor age, has always been half angel, half devil, will at last fulfill its original promise of being a demigod on wheels.

NOTES

[1] In Gyorgy Kepes, ed., *Sign Image Symbol* (New York, 1966), p. 87.

[2] See B.A. Botkin, " 'Folk-Say' and Folklore," *American Speech,* VI (August, 1931), 404-406.

[3] Acel Garland, "Songs of Yesterday and Today," *Folk-Say, A Regional Miscellany,* edited by B. A. Botkin (Norman, Okla., 1929), pp. 96-97. For an early study of automobile folksay and slang see George Milburn, "The Tax Talk," *Ibid.,* pp. 108-112.

[4] Dick Wick Hall, Editor and Miner, *Salome Sun,* Vols. 1 and 3, 1921, 1922. For a study of automobile humor see B. A. Botkin, "Automobile Humor: From the Horseless Carriage to the Compact Car," *Journal of Popular Culture,* I, Spring, 1968, pp. 395-402.

[5] Fanya Del Bourgo, "Love in the City," as told to B.A. Botkin, *New York Folklore Quarterly, XXI,* Sept. 1965, pp. 170,178.

[6] Bellamy Partridge, *Fill 'er Up!* (New York, 1952), pp. 189, 190.

[7] Waldo Frank, *In the American Jungle,* New York, 1937, p. 50.

[8] Grace and Fred M. Hechinger, "Serious Epidemic of 'Automania,' " *The New York Times Magazine,* August 11, 1963, p. 18.

[9] Robert H. Boyle, "The Car Cult from Rumpsville," *Sports Illustrated,* April 24, 1961, pp. 70-71.

[10] Ken W. Purdy's *Wonderful World of the Automobile,* (New York, 1960,) pp. 26 ff.

[11] Robert H. Boyle, *op,cit.,* p. 83.

[12]Harold D. Leslie, "Harold and the Green Dragon," *Petroleum Today,* IV, Spring, 1963, p. 6.

[13]Robert H. Boyle, *op. cit.,* p. 79.

THE IMAGE IN AMERICAN LIFE: VOLKSWAGEN

by

Harry Hammond

THE IMAGE IN AMERICAN LIFE: VOLKSWAGEN

by

Harry Hammond

The ultimate in the democratic car was the creation of one of the more undemocratic leaders of all time. The People's Car was one of Adolf Hitler's pet projects. Americans laughed at his dream in the late thirties. Now they pay around two thousand dollars to buy one. This is irony on a grand scale, the spectacle of over two million Volkswagens puttering around the country that saved the world from Hitler.

Obviously, pro or anti German sentiment had little effect on the popularity of the Volkswagen over the years. Hitler's three hundred ninety-six dollar Strength-Through-Joy flivver enjoyed an early revamping of its image unaccompanied by the repackaging we would have expected. The British reluctantly decided to patch up

the bombed-out Wolfsburg factory more out of desperation than
enthusiasm. The few cars that wobbled off the post war line were
near duplicates of Ferdinand Porsche's 1936 prototypes.

   Volkswagen came on the American scene in 1948.
Henry Ford's decision that year to not accept the British offer of
the VW plant coincided with the appointment of Heinz Nordhoff
to gear up production. Ford had only a few years to feel comfortable
with that decision. Though the company failed to enlist American
dealers in 1948 and 1949, by the close of 1950 they had convinced
a New York foreign car dealer to sign on as the exclusive Volkswagen
agent for the United States. The 330 cars sold in America that year
were the beginning of the "bug invasion," the Detroit image of Volkswagen exports to·this country.

   The response in Detroit was predictable. Denunciation,
accompanied by flag waving and followed by imitation helped the
VW rather than hurt it. Comparison ads rallied attention to the
opponent, a blunder considering the masses of chrome happy Americans previously unaware of the industry infighting. But then the very
assumption that the crippling blow could be dealt through advertising
was a misreading of the VW's success pattern.

   Recent estimates show Volkswagen ads have twice the
readership of any other automobile ads in America. Prior to 1957,
surprisingly, the VW people had not even begun their blissful affair
with Doyle Dane Bernbach, the agency responsible for institutionalizing
slick page understatement. The VW ad did not create the Volkswagen.
Understandably, Detroit's advertising defensive did nothing more than
help VW sales.

   It was American Motors who spearheaded (they're proud
to say) the "Buy American" movement in the auto industry. Recent
television commercials portray the bugs swarming over the land of
the free–which happens also to be the land of the Rambler. This
attempt at infecting the entire American public with the Detroit
strain of Volksphobia had its precedent for failure in the late forties
and early fifties. Articles in *Nation, Life, Newsweek* and *Popular
Science* were headlined "Herr Tin Lizzie; the Volkswagen," "Volkswagen, go home!", "Adolf's little auto," "Hitler's flivver, now sold

in the U.S." Underlining of this Führer—VW association led the company to launch a defense campaign. Internationalizing the car's image was the tact. In America they worked to convince the public that it is "buying American" to sink your money in a Volkswagen. Success once again was theirs. Last May I was lectured on import-export, balance of trade and dollar credits on the European money market. A retired farmer had me a captive audience on the way to cut asparagus (mode of transportation: VW, of course).

Nearly everyone in Detroit has soiled their hands through imitation. The trend is cyclical. Success, declining sales, and phase-out is the pattern. Often this includes an intermediate stage of growth in the model's physical dimensions. The Rambler American has done well at American Motors. Yet Chevrolet's Corvair bit the dust in late 1968. With its engine in the rear the Corvair was the obvious pretender. At Ford the Falcon grew bigger and bigger with the years and is now joined by its smaller cousin the Maverick. Now these are all splendid products. Their limited successes have not been due to any superior qualities of the VW. Their disappointing sales records are merely the compliment of Volkswagen success.

There is only one argument that attempts to explain the steel bug's sales victory. Many VW devotees have told me that buying the bug is an affirmation of common sense, where common sense takes precedence over sentiment, where desire for the practical over-rides anti-Nazi feelings and flag waving inclinations. The company uses the same line. Nordhoff has said, "The Volkswagen supplies a need which American production doesn't."

Walter Henry Nelson elaborates this thinking in his book *Small Wonder, The Amazing Story of the Volkswagen.* His work is of the "a VW is built and one is sold every eight seconds" genre. Keep it in mind as a corporate history, celebrating the tragedies of Porsche, the triumphs of Nordhoff and the vigor of the Wolfsburg population, all set off by the chorous of continually rising production figures. "The 5,000,000 car." Gloria!

But praise says little to us. What is the significance of this Germanese beetle in America? Obviously the success of the Volkswagen in Germany (where it is after all German) or in Brazil (where its competition has legs) does not explain the impact of the VW on American life.

The fiction of the "supplies a demand" argument is the assumption that a savings of several hundred dollars would be enough to make two million Americans buy German. Several hundred dollars might be the decisive factor for those with low incomes. A tour of your local slums would make that consideration meaningless. Low incomes types in the United State shy away from the People's car.

Neither advertising nor American demand explain the Small Wonder. Everyone wishes it were that simple. Wolfsburg production managers, the staff at Englewood Cliffs, N.J. (VW of America Headquarters), Detroit, Madison Avenue, who wouldn't feel threatened with the possibility of the VW being a mystery?

Bringing coals to Newcastle has long been one example of the absurd. Detroit has long regarded the bug as coal. Yet the phenomenon of the VW is absurd only so far as it has been unexplained Temporary, experimental and bizarre are concepts associated with the Volkswagen. We may laugh with the West Germans or run a fever with the board room gang in Detroit as we choose. But as Pop Culturists we have to look into the impact of this car. Its impression, friends, is everywhere. The U-boat, subject of serious works, was a disaster for America. The Volkswagen, subject of only whimsical treatments, is probably not a disaster. Then what is it?

The story of invention, leadership and sales promotion treats the business history of the product. But to recognize the product as a significant cultural object is to ask other questions. What does the Volkswagen say as a social document? What is the behavioral history of the car-owner unit on the American scene. Work in this area would focus on some of the following episodes:

1. Volkswagen Club of America organized, 1952 (publishers of the *VW Autoist*).

2. Civil suit brought by U.S. Department of Justice

against Volkswagen of America in an attempt to end the practices of price fixing and exclusive franchises.

3.   Sargent Shriver compares his Peace Corps to the VW (continue to improve. . . same externally).

4.   The "volkstote" (team carry VW and drive it back) replaces cramming as most popular campus bug event.

5.   Volkslore (VW humor and anecdotes) sells big.

6.   Robert Kennedy makes news campaigning through an open sunroof of a VW.

7.   Metric tools appear on Woolworths' counters (already standard in Sears catalog, along with rebuilt VW engines).

8.   John Lennon (the other kind of Beatle) buys one.

9.   Ralph Nader (self-appointed consumer's watchdog) attacks the VW.

10.   Springmaid Fabrics bring out a Volkswagen print for blouses.

11.   Creative Playthings catalog shows the VW as representative car in its transportation toys.

12.   Subara (Japanese car) advertisements read "Cheap, Ugly, Economical."

13.   Wink (soda) sponsors a "Paint your wagon" contest. Decorate an outline of a VW and win the real thing.

14.   Walt Disney Productions film *The Love Bug,* a
movie about Herbie, the VW.

A look into the object as cultural text must also reflect the feedback
influence on the object itself. What of America's effect on the car?
The continued emphasis on the standard model is related to that
model's sales volume in the United States. Whenever the company
introduces a new model (the 411L is now making its debut in Germany)
sales are restricted. This must be read as a conscious effort to support
the timeless image of the beetle shape in America. Only later, and
then gradually, do new models circulate in the American market.
Other American influences on the car are the footpedals re-designed
for women, the variety of colors, and the raised bumber. Ironically,
the very concept of the People's Car originated with Henry Ford.
Even the first VW prototypes had doors which opened from the
rear, another lesson Ferdinand Porsche learned from his study of
the American industry.

Part of the VW's image comes from the constant myth-
making activities of Volkswagen of America. Their creative tools
are effective, especially the magazine *Small World.* The Editors
reprint articles from other magazines or books that add to the approved
official image. Best among them are Tom Wolfe's "Why Doormen
Hate Volkswagens," adapted from his book *The Kandy Kolored
Tangerine-Flake Streamline Baby,* and Arnold Gingrich's "My Affair
with the Volkswagen," reprinted from *Esquire.* Most issues of
Small World feature departments such as "Driving it Right," "Small
Talk," and "Care and Feeding." The editors do a good job, carefully
balancing each issue with Leters to the Editor that complain as well
as laud.

Another front in the image battle is the free distribution
of VW jokes and anecdotes to newspapers, and the awarding of savings
bonds (U.S. of course) to ladies who have babies in the back seat of
their VW's. In addition, the organization publicizes the social life of
Volkswagens everywhere. Stop by your dealer for a reprint of the
Sports Illustrated article that proves they float.

A more subtle method of controlling the VW image is

the tight grasp the parent company holds on its 3,000 dealers. Number of work stalls each must have is specified, as are the types of desk salesmen are to use, and even the way posters are to be framed for display. Nelson recounts the story of the New Hampshire dealer who talked with prospective customers while sitting casually cross-legged on the floor. It sold cars but also provoked the VW hierarchy. This dealer now stands erect and tidy. A film, *The Right Hand of Plenty,* rounds out the story of the image machine.

Words like wholesome, practical, All-American, honest, simple—we all know the list—evoke the image the company peddles. But that is not to say it is company created. That image is to some extent determined by the public's image. And that in turn grows partly from the individuals who both learn from the prior image and help create the present one.

These individuals, the buyers and the drivers are the proper subject of investigation. What are the components of that asparagus farmer's VW image? Can we explain the Volkswagen in terms of image, value and cult?

My local Ford dealer wasn't shook at all when told "I'm seriously considering a VW, instead of the Falcon." In a casual, practiced manner he led me over to a set of plush chairs (in the shadow of Old Glory), gave an understanding smile, then began the character assassination that to an American is no news at all. Anyone can tell you that the Volkswagen oversteers, the heating is lousy, the horn beepy, the brakes squeaky, and the cross-wind behavior scandalous. Rowing the transmission lever of a VW is also as American as apple pie. Every car salesman at some point in his career must face the customer walking the fence that seperates the bugged minority from others. His performance on those occasions has a ritual quality about it that reminds me of the even more ritualistic behavior of VW owners.

The constituency of the Volkswagen faithful reflects variety of class, age, interest and degree of devotion. Devotion, even worship, are not overstatements in describing some owner behavior. I've seen them being waxed, weekly. Pest control people may dress their bugs as mice (as in Miami) and many agree with one owner who thought VWs were like soft shelled crabs, simply a matter of taste.

But for every VW with a pin wheel or wind-up key on the rear there is one which enjoys a relationship with his owner that resembles that of a horse to its cowboy.

More womblike than phallic, the Volkswagen is something you wear, get into to share. The VW is accessory not weapon. One teacher, uneasy with the racial problems at her inner city high school, confessed she feels Negroes who drive VWs seem more friendly. Marshall McLuhan's discussion of the "totem image" is intriguing. Is the Volkswagen one of those straightjackets that permit the owner to relate to the world? Most informants have referred to their bugs as highly personal. Often names are dropped, even unconsciously (Betsy, Algernon, Harry, Petunia, etc.).

The Volkswagen illustrates rather than exhibits life style. The display is casual, low-keyed, not often self-consciously put-on. Some people do psychologically climb into VW skins. Why is not so clear. Another variety of VW fan is the Formula Vee racer (VW engines on tubular racing chassis). This character deliberately adorns himself with the style of his machine. Speed, competition, show are indications that his association with the car is temporary and calculated, at least partially for effect. But the typical owner is more in tune with the man who said, "I never wax her. I don't know that I'll ever want to trade up to a newer one. You get used to each other." This guy has a rapport with his car that is characterized by quiet devotion, even ritual. The specific car evokes a response. Like the Disney creation Herbie, it has personality.

It is possible, of course, that the data I've been gathering from informal conversations weights the exceptional. Is the guy who won't "trade up" as rare a bird as the enthusiast who goes in for flared rear fenders and needle bearing rocker arms? There have been those who recite the official image. For them the car's main feature is economy. It retains value, exhibits good workmanship and is fun to drive. The People's Car becomes the people's panacea. Fed-up-ism inspires the search for basic car instead of the usual Detroit pleasure barge. But the unusual amount of agreement within this group makes one suspicious. Such superficial homogeneity can be credited to at least three possibilities.

First, my information gathering technique was at fault. My work has been a casual exploration. Conversation with owners caught many unprepared and even more uninterested. No doubt some found it easier to repeat the last Doyle Dane Bernbach ad and be rid of me.

Secondly, it might be a case of super sales success. But we've already seen that Volkswagen was big in America even before Doyle Dane and Bernbach came on the scene. And the proven qualities of the smaller American cars, coupled with Detroit's generous and also clever advertising, rule for dismissal of this possibility.

The third possibility is that both the unexplained sales success of Hitler's dream car and the unexplained homogenized-plus image are signs of factors at work on another level. Are Americans compulsively, perhaps unconsciously, responding to vague public dreams or symbols?

We may not be able to arrange the "why" scale of the Volkswagen's presence until after it passes. Though I expect the bug will be with us long after it becomes absurd to use it. Like the penknife in the executive's pocket, or Granddad's watch in its plastic dome, the Volkswagen might be one of those icons we, as a culture, clutch, often long after utility rules them useless.

SEMI–ANNUAL INSTALLMENT ON
THE AMERICAN DREAM: THE WISH
BOOK AS POPULAR ICON

by

Fred E. H. Schroeder

SEMI—ANNUAL INSTALLMENT ON THE AMERICAN DREAM: THE WISH BOOK AS POPULAR ICON

by

Fred E. H. Schroeder

In wishful moments an archaeologist must dream of unearthing in Greece a *Searsopolis Roebuckeles Katalog* or its equivalent
in Egypt, Mexico, South Africa or Turkestan. At times the culture-
diggers have come close to this dream, as in the tomb of Tutankhamen,
but this is more akin to unearthing an encyclopedia of what a culture
planned to be remembered by than it is a candid catalog of everyday
Egyptian life. Archaeologists have little to go on in studying earlier
cultures, and it is remarkable how few artifacts and remains it takes
to keep them happy. A cuneiform table of royal accounts, a broken
clay head from Tlatilco, an occipital ridge and a molar from Olduvai,
rotted postholes from an Ohio moundbuilder's stockade; these representative fragments will yield notes in archaeological journals, a

few Ph.D.s, and a slight broadening and deepening of our images of
past civilizations.

Much more could be learned from disinterred mail-order
catalogs, if the archaeologist's fanciful wish were granted. We would
learn not only of the garments of men, women, and children, but of
their undergarments as well; not only of the homes of the culture,
but of the tools and materials which went to make those homes; not
only of how things and people were measured and made, but of how
they were maintained and repaired with the equivalents of glues and
trusses, paints and tampons, auto tune-up manuals and Bibles, hydraul
jacks and vitamin pills. Even more: the archaeologist could tell us
of the self-images and wishes of everyday men and women. He could
gain for us a window on their worlds of realities and dreams.

In that respect the mail-order catalog is truly an Americar
icon. In the most traditional sense, of course, the word *icon* is applied
to the religious images of Byzantium. "To the Byzantines," the
historian D.A. Miller tells us, "the icon was the physical memorandum
of something beyond; the window (the term is often used) through
which men may look into higher realms."[1] The Byzantine icons
with which most of us are familiar are mosaics, pieced together of
glittering fragments. The personages depicted in them are conven-
tionalized to the point of being quite indistinguishable from one
another, and the rendering of perspective, size and color violate
scientific realism in the quest for the higher reality of "something
beyond." In addition, the icons were popular works of art for the
Byzantine masses, not for the aristocrats, whose art was in the private
world of illuminated books.[2] But to the average Byzantine, all these
apparent shortcomings were dissolved in the immediacy of the total
impression.

The American catalog is remarkably similar, even to the
irreverently reverent nicknames by which Americans express the
mystical function of their icons:*The Wish Book, The Big Book, The
Farmers' Bible.*[3] Although each Big Book is a hefty unit, it is mosaic
in structure, every item a glittering, if fragmentary, contribution to
the totality. Even the "reverse perspective" of Byzantine art whereby
psychological and spiritual importance dictate relative size and bril-

liance is reflected in the catalog-page layout. Thus, in the Montgomery Ward 1968 Christmas catalog, the "Family Reference Bible" is larger than "young people's" or "study" Bibles.[4] This technique, as well as the family emphasis, is as old as the catalogs, for the 1897 Sears Roebuck catalog shows the "Family Sunshine Range"[5] and the "Home Sunshine Range"[6] looming heavily over the spiritually diminutive "Othello" range and crass laundry stoves. Further, despite the fact that for nearly fifty years the catalog clothing has been photographed on living models, their faces and bodies are so nearly indistinguishable (including the recently added Afro-and Oriental-Americans) that it is difficult to recognize the same model in different costumes and poses. The models, like icon Christs, classical Greek statues, and Gibson's girls are conventional representations of the Ideal, not breathing individual beings. Readers of *Vogue* may identify with bony individualists, but catalog readers find the American Ideal in well-nourished equalitarians who transcend the ego. Not only are the models dissolved in mosaic anonymity, but the catalog writers and photographers are as nameless as the artists of the old icons.

But to draw such technical parallels between traditional icons and mail-order catalogs is hardly more than a clever game. Is it fair and honest to extend these parallels to the totality? The Byzantine icon exists for a spiritual purpose. Is it valid to equate a material price-list with a spiritual symbol? To borrow from the argot of computer sales, the icon is a medium of software while the catalog is apparently no more than a material means to a hardware end. The icon unquestionably embodies the spiritual values of the culture. Does the catalog do this too? And if it does, what dismally material meaning does it give to our culture?

To get at answers to these questions, it is first necessary to recognize that the spirituality of an icon is not inherent to the object as such. That is, the object is an icon only to one who sees it as an image that means something to him. Hence, the Byzantine icon is not truly an icon to those of us who are not heirs to Byzantine Christianity. While the term is a convenient tag for discussing these objects as a class of artworks, they are not our icons. They are *things* to us, not meanings. Every culture, in this sense, has its own peculiar icons which will appear as mere things, not as meanings, to people of other cultures. The fact that the catalog is itself a material thing of things does not prevent its being an image of loftier meanings.

The mail-order catalog does have meanings to Americans. It is the Wish Book; it is the semi-annual installment on the American Dream. More: it is the semi-annual *affirmation* of the American Dream, because the catalog's Wishes and Dreams are thrown out every six months, like an accelerated version of primitive societies' annual death and rebirth of a god. It is the paradox of "the king is dead; long live the king." But few gods and kings have such ignominious and unceremonious ends as mail-order catalogs, which variously go out with the trash, kindle stove fires, are cut up for paperdolls, or drop, page by page, into rural privy pits. At the rare times that an old catalog is found or reprinted, it is regarded as an object of affectionate ridicule, not of reverence. There is not room in the American mind for yesterday's dreams any more than there is for yesterday's automobile. "Old deeds for old people," said that arch-enemy of materialism, Henry Thoreau, "new deeds for new"; and the catalog echoes, "old things for old people, and new things for new." Thus, from the earliest of the catalogs to the present, there have been few pages given to old things. The 1897 Sears catalog has no period furniture; and although the 1969 catalog does—even in 1908 the catalog carried "Roman" chairs—[7] it is because it is new to be old, particularly with such new transformations as: "COLONIAL BAR. . .Black vinyl spill rail and decorative panels padded with polyurethane"[8]. . ."Grandma's 19th Century styling here with these 20th Century features *Large automatic oven *Built-in rotisserie. . .Low as $279.95 cash electric. . . ."[9]

Popular icons are sometimes discernible by the folklore which surrounds them, but, strangely, although there are catalog tales, they have been neither collected nor indexed.[10] This is probably true because the mail-order catalogs are so intimately contemporary to most Americans' experiences. There must exist an infinity of catalog-in-the-outhouse jokes and fabliaux of elementary lessons in sex gleaned from the underclothing and pharmacy pages, but these tales apparently are too close to everyday American experience to warrant transmutation into fantasy and folklore. That is, the anecdotes which are current are simply factual recitations of individual occurrences which rather than being passed on as lore, serve only to evoke other factual anecdotes. For example, one mail-order customer's experience of a back-order delay is likely to be regarded as only slightly different from another customer's having been sent the wrong item. There is little raw material for fantasy and fiction at Wards and Sears, for, like a chess game, everything is aboveboard. Horsetrading and traveling salesmanship, like politics and poker, are richly productive of folklore, because there is enough hidden underhand to permit the development of fiction. But the whole mail-order catalog experience is above board, and the whole tradition is based on mutual trust. What few anecdotes there are about catalogs are stories which express some deviation from straightforward, aboveboard trust. Sometimes the deviation is on the part of the mail-order house, but since these errors are almost invariably rectified, they are not productive of any particularly lasting lore.

More often the deviation from aboveboard straightforward trust takes the form of trusting the catalog and the mail-order house beyond reason. Thus, when a Sunday-school teacher asks, "Where did Moses get the Ten Commandments?" and the pupil replies "From Sears Roebuck,"[11] the child's trust exceeds the aboveboard contract which the mail-order catalog is in reality. Adult consumers as well have been known to carry their trust to extremes. Shortly after the turn of the century, a customer dropped his Sears Roebuck watch on a sidewalk, and when it broke, he wrote to the company to complain. The request for a refund was shown to Richard Warren Sears who directed: "Write him that our watches are guaranteed not to fall on concrete sidewalks; and send him a new watch."[12]

Trust is the essence of the mail-order catalog business, and that is one respect in which the catalog of material things is the icon of an abstract ideal, because there is an equalitarian dignity implied in such catholic reciprocity of trust between an institution and the masses. The credit for starting the tradition is due to Aaron Montgomery Ward, whose simple idea was to buy directly from manufacturers for cash and to sell directly to farmers, also for cash,

and at a very low markup. His first "catalog" in 1872 was a single
sheet. Two years later it had eight pages and bore the first true
mail-order guarantee, that all items were sent by express "subject
to examination."[13] The most extreme version of the guaranteed
trust was Richard Sears' "Send No Money" campaign, which began
in 1900. Sears had entered the general mail-order business by way
of watches which he sold at low enough prices that they could be
resold at a profit. By 1892, when Ward's catalog had expanded to
over 500 pages and his gross income exceeded $1,000,000 Sears
had given over half his catalog to goods other than watches and
jewelry. Until 1900, goods were sold for cash, although Sears invited
his customers to send their payments to his Minneapolis bankers, to
be turned over to Sears only if they trusted him. Under the "Send
No Money" agreement, orders were sent Collect On Delivery, but
by 1902, with almost $800,000 worth of unclaimed and returned
merchandise—and catalogs in the hands of virtually the entire rural
population of the United States— Sears abandoned the practice,
returning to the requirement that cash accompany the order.[14]
The "Send No Money" technique is still a valued means of winning
trust and expanding markets, however, since in recent years the
Spiegel firm, looking for a larger slice of the mail-order business, has
employed a variation on Sears' old method.

The trust which Montgomery Ward and Richard Sears
wanted to win from Americans was based on their knowledge of and
respect for the shrewd and well-founded suspicion which farmers held
for local merchants, who often operated without competition and took
advantage of their monopolies. The catalogs strived to become entirely
trustworthy. From the beginning, the pictures and descriptions of
the items are enticing, but they are not exaggerated. Julius Rosenwald,
who later succeeded Sears, and the first regular catalog editor, William
Pettigrew,[15]began the "healthy custom of calling skunk fur 'Skunk'
and dyed rabbit 'Dyed Rabbit'," and of giving actual volume of
kitchen utensils, and of guaranteeing horsepower of motors and
engines.[16] The verbal honesty is exemplary. In a 1937 review of
the Sears catalog in *The Saturday Review of Literature*, Lovell
Thompson wrote that "Sears offered free to American writers. . .a

model of style. . .conscientious, frank, direct; it is hard to doubt the truth of what is said. . . . Sears knows the precise word when you don't."[17]

Honest, aboveboard, precise wording is the essence of the catalogs' literary style. Very early, "copywriters were instructed to say 'sweat,' not 'perspiration;' 'go to bed,' not 'retire;' 'food,' not 'nutrition;' 'tears,' not 'lachrymal secretions;' and 'men and women' instead of 'ladies and gents.' Also taboo became phrases such as 'lowest prices in America,' 'world's largest dealer in lawn-mowers,' 'America's stongest work pants,' unless justified by actual fact."[18] Precise wording in the modern catalogs includes unequivocal definitions of such terms as "sunfast," "preshrunk," "sanforized," "linear poly-ethylene," "DTU" and "automatic frequency control."[19] Catalog terminology has even served to standardize the American language, as people in the provinces are obliged to order pictured items in the dialect of the Chicago-centered mail-order houses. What is still known in the rural South as a "sling-blade" or "slam-bang" must be ordered from a picture labelled "weed cutter."[20] Apropos to standardizing, it is undoubtedly true that the acceptance by mail-order houses in 1941 of the age-size standards developed by the U.S. Bureau of Home Economics from WPA statistics was a major force in placing competing stores and manufacturers on an equal basis in stating sizes;[21] just as the catalogs were the force which accustomed Americans to the one-price retail system rather than the old traditional marked-price-asking-price-selling-price system.[22] In these and other ways, the mail-order catalogs have become intimately woven into the very fabric of American life.

There are some snarled spots in the fabric, however. The values expressed by this icon are not all positive. On the retail level, the catalogs reflect the perennial American quarrel between nationalism and regionalism. The nationalizing threat of the catalogs was fought by local merchants who saw the catalogs as instruments to draw money out of town, although they themselves bought their goods from out of town wholesalers. Consequently, loyal rural and small town consumers bought from the catalogs with a feeling of guilt. In 1903, Richard W. Sears promised to ease the guilt by re-

fraining from placing his firm's name on any "box, package, wrapper,
tag, envelope or article of merchandise."[23] The merchants countered
by spreading rumors of cheap quality goods,[24] by telling jokes about
one-dollar mail-order sewing machines that turned out on arrival to
be a needle and a spool of thread,[25] and, in the South, by promoting
whisper campaigns rumoring that Richard Warren Sears was a Negro.[26]
Another snarl in the fabric which disturbs the big mail-order houses
today is the "hick" stigma which remains from pre-war years, when
catalogs were almost exclusively directed toward rural needs. In the
depression year of 1937, the Sears Spring and Summer catalog cover
exemplified the sales target of their catalog by depicting a wholesome
young couple on a hilltop overlooking their John Steuart Curry farm.
Reviewing this catalog as "Eden in Easy Payments," Lovell Thompson
regarded it as a "guide to rural America" with "New York. . .the
serpent in Sears' garden."[27] Today, however, all the major catalogs
direct their sales campaigns toward the serpents; yet the hick stigma
is still discernible both in the tone of bravado and in the rational
apologies (footnoted from that icon of sciencism, *Consumer Reports)*
which are employed by urbanites who have bought goods from one
of the catalogs or one of their modern retail outlets. These retail
stores, incidentally, are not to be regarded as icons, for, like the J.C.
Penney stores and A&P supermarkets, the retail stores are too public,
too tied to personalities and local associations to be icons. The
catalog, on the other hand, is a househeld window looking out upon
things beyond the local horizon.

The pre-World War II catalog did indeed represent a
bucolic Garden of Eden; but the urban-directed post-war catalogs,
the expansion of the chains of retail stores, and ultimately, the additio
of such sophisticated new lines as "designer" clothes and original
art works in the 1960s marked a social reversal. To retain the Edenic
image, the Garden of Eden invaded the very atelier of the serpent,
New York City. The Garden remained strangely innocent, for art,
clothing and furniture in the catalog never became confused with
class-consciousness. The catalogs remained books of *things*, and
the things remained achievable, all clearly marked with an unambivalen
price-tag, all clearly designated as Good, Better or Best in material

quality. Even in the serpentine metropolis, every man enters the catalog's Eden on equal footing. Things may have different prices, but one man's dollar is as good as another's. Such classless ideals do not enhance snobbery.

In assuaging the guilt about hick-stigma, Sears Roebuck has been most resourceful in fighting fire with fire, by converting the out-of-date to the nostalgic; but, in addition to wiring "Grandma's stove," selling reproductions of 1897 catalog pocket-watches, and (in 1968) baldly labelling their Christmas catalog a "Wish Book"-- including in it such urbanely wished-for items as a $1600 suit of Toledo armor and a $3300 diamond pendant-- Sears has engaged as "consultants" Sir Edmund Hillary and Vincent Price. The Vincent Price art collection was not Sears' first foray into the art field, nor was it a sudden leap into high-quality aesthetics. In 1944, a year in which more than two hundred items were listed as unavailable due to war shortages, Sears offered canvas finish oil-painting reproductions of famous American paintings, including George Inness' *Peace and Plenty* which also served as the cover illustration.[28] The Sears Fall and Winter catalog in 1969 offered only five art reproductions (at $5.99 and $9.99, exquisitely framed), but one can hardly go wrong aesthetically with well-selected works by Rembrandt, Fragonard, Cezanne, Van Gogh and Picasso. Similarily, when the Vincent Price mail-order collection of original prints was introduced in 1963, no one could question the quality of the selections. Nonetheless, Frank Getlein, writing in the *New Republic,* seemed to feel that some cheapening of fine art had occurred. This may not have been his intended meaning, for his prose, unlike that of the catalogs, has a serpentine ambiguity and scaly irony. Sears "pays art the supreme mercantile compliment of treating it as merchandise," he wrote. "The art of Sears seems to come under the homefurnishings depart-ment, as it does for the vast majority of Americans who ever buy a print or painting. . . ."[29]

Which brings us back to the mail-order catalog's office as popular icon. An icon should be a "window through which men may look into higher realms" at the same time that it embodies es-sential values of its culture. The surface values of American culture

expressed in the Wish Book are values of material well being, of middle
class equality and of democratic mutual respect. There is another,
profounder, value which grows out of these others. Alexis de Tocque-
ville identified it and named it "indefinite perfectibility." This is
the higher realm on which the catalog provides a window. The
material things are there,   and they are achievable. All things achievable bear a price-tag, even works of art, and all can be labelled Good
or Better or Best, despite the fact that today's Best may be demoted
to tomorrow's Better. Such is the way of indefinite perfectibility.
In six months there will be a new window on even higher realms of
material well being. And that well being will be attainable, too.
Even as early in catalog history as 1917, *Scribner's* magazine extolled
the moral honesty of the catalog's "quiet, steadying mission" to be
concerned "frankly with mere things." Within these limits, the catalog
"does not set us longing for more than we can possibly buy,"[30] nor
does it make a claim to purveying the things that money cannot buy.
The catalog sells Bibles, not salvation. The catalog sells Best quality
trousers, not best quality taste. The catalog sells genuine art works,
not genuine taste.

      The *New Republic's* comments on the mail-order sales
of original Rembrandts, Callots, Whistlers and Calders suggest a con-
flict in values. If art is not merchandise, if art is not homefurnishings,
then what is it? If art is not for home and family, if it is not *things*
like the Family Sunshine Range or the Family Reference Bible, what
transcendent no-thing can art be? Is art only for kings and aristocrats?
But the American Dream is the one that Huey Long reduced to a
slogan: every man a king. Hence, if art is for kings, art is presumably
for every American. Or, is art to be revered and viewed only on
sabbath afternoons in secular temples? To do so is to revere things,
not ideals, and the catalog-icon resists the whole idea of reverence for
material things. Artworks, stoves, Bibles and mail-order catalogs
are themselves things, material, transitory and replaceable. Thus, it
is a paradoxical possibility that the catalogs of things, resting on a
tradition of mutual trust, help American consumers to distinguish
between material things that money can buy and higher **values** that
money cannot. The trust, once destroyed, could not be replaced;

the catalog can be replaced. Wards, Sears, Spiegels, Penneys and Aldens deliver the goods, but should they cease to deliver the goods, reverence will not prevent iconoclasm. Old icons for old men; new icons for new.

The mail-order catalog, then, is an American popular icon for more reasons than its mosaic structure. Intertwined in the fabric of daily life, it influences basic behavior patterns of domestic economy and of language, and, most of all it fulfills the quasi-religious function of providing an affirmation of the attainment of the dream of those who emigrated to America; a dream of sharing equally in the material produce of the society. Patterns of deeper meanings, infinitely complex, are discernible as well. The icon is classless, yet distinguishes between the old, which is obsolete and outcaste, and the new, which must be kept new in semi-annual reincarnations. Unlike most ritual reaffirmations, this icon is different in every re-birth. The unfathomable paradox of the American mind is that the unchanging value is change itself. The carrot moves before the donkey, the fruit eternally eludes Tantalus, and the mail-order catalog draws Americans forward with wishes of something better. But the wish-function of the catalog passeth all understanding, for its wishes are attainable. It is true, of course, that all Americans cannot buy all they wish for, just as it is regrettably true that all Americans do not share equally in the nation's well being. The catalog rests on an assumed general equality, and the assumption is not ill-founded, for some of its goods will be found in homes on Indian reservations, in Appalachian cabins and in urban slums. For the Americans in these places, the icon function of the Wish Book is intensified, not denied. Finally, and compounding all the other paradoxes, is the apparent fact that the uncompromising materialism of the icon and its mosaic bits reassure consumers of eternal spiritual values; that is, there *are* things that money cannot buy. Those things, the icon means, cannot be reissued in newer, better forms every six months.

Returning at last to the possibility of mail-order catalogs for past civilizations, it is clear that the speculation is fanciful because the mail-order catalog is at once image and product of the uniquely American experience. This is true not only for this popular icon, but

it is true in the higher arts, where cataloging is a style of nationalistic
expression which has been employed by such artists as Walt Whitman,
Hart Crane and Charles Ives to evoke the sweep and conflicting
variousness of the unity which is America. Even more, the speculation
is fanciful because the very concept of the Wish Book is posited on
the achievement of one of the great wishes of mankind, the wish
for universal literacy. Without universal literacy there could be no
book of material wishes for the masses of men and women. The
Wish Book of things is reserved for those fortunate people whose
three magic wishes have already been granted: democracy, literacy
and reciprocal trust.

NOTES

[1] *The Byzantine Tradition.* Harper and Row, 1966, p. 75.

[2] Andre Grabar, *Byzantine Painting.* Skira, 1953, p. 34.

[3] On the plains, as recently as 1921, it was called the "home-
steaders' *Bible"* Viola I.Paradise, "By Mail" *Scribner's,* April, 1921, p.473.

[4] Grabar, p. 153.

[5] Fred I. Israel, editor. Chelsea House Publishers, 1968, p.122.

[6] *Ibid.,* p. 124.

[7] Joseph J. Schroeder, Jr., editor. Gun Digest Company, 1969,
p. 376.

[8] Spring and Summer, 1969, p. 1417.

[9] *Ibid., p. 845.*

[10] There are no anecdotes, sayings or jokes indexed in such
standard sources as *The Journal of American Folklore,* B.A. Botkin's *Treasury
of American Anecdotes,* Ralph Woods' *Modern Handbook of Humor* or Evan
Esar's *20,000 Quips and Jokes.*

[11] Viola I. Paradise, "By Mail," *Scribner's,* April, 1921, p. 480.

[12] Louis E. Asher and Edith Heal, *Send No Money.* Argus, 1942, p. 9.

[13] Boris Emmet and John E. Jeuck, *Catalogs and Counters. A History of Sears, Roebuck and Company.* University of Chicago Press, 1950, pp. 20-21.

[14] Asher and Heal, pp. 52-53; Emmet and Jueck, pp. 23-31.

[15] Emmet and Jueck, pp. 97-98.

[16] Edward Earle Purinton, "Satisfaction or Your Money Back," *Independent,* February 21, 1920, p. 297.

[17] "Eden in Easy Payments," April 3, 1937, p. 15.

[18] Emmet and Jueck, p. 252.

[19] Montomery Ward Fall and Winter, 1969, p. 1422; Sears, Roebuck Fall and Winter, 1969, pp. 738-739.

[20] Sears, Roebuck Spring and Summer, 1969, p. 1079.

[21] "Fitting Willie's Suit," *Business Week,* April 5,1941, pp.38-39.

[22] George Milburn, "Catalogues and Culture," *Good Housekeeping* April , 1946, pp. 183-184.

[23] Asher and Heal, p. 108.

[24] *Ibid.,* pp. 105-106.

[25] Emmet and Jueck, p. 44.

[26] Asher and Heal p. 5n.

[27] *Saturday Review of Literature,* April 3,1937, pp. 15-16.

[28]"Sears Offers Art," *Business Week,* July 8,1944, p. 95.

[29] "Art at Sears," April 20,1963, p. 27.

[30]"Point of View," April, 1917, p. 512.

THE MISSING IMAGE

by

Sam Rosenberg

THE MISSING IMAGE

by

Sam Rosenberg

Like most of the objects we see and handle every day, the match-box label is invisible. We read its message without seeing the words of the message or the design of the label. Usually we open the box, take out the match, light our cigarette and put away the box without any recollection of the box itself. It takes a strikingly new or odd design, or a touch of schizophrenia to get the message from a commonplace object and to see it, too.

Hundreds of things have become invisible in this sense. The pencil, the letters on the printed page, shoes, buttons, the chair, the table, the telephone. We step outside and fail to see the buildings, the cars, the fire hydrants or the people walking on the street. Our

enveloping daydreams and the interminable cinema we call consciousness mask out all other visions. Even the face and body of
the beloved one become seen-unseen, visible and invisible. Sometimes
we are genuinely startled to see our own faces in the bathroom mirror.

But that is not all. The famous spiller of ink, Doctor
Rorschach, has been the latest expert to draw attention to the fact
that when we do look hard at something we tend to see *something
else instead!* I remember the consternation created by a young
Lieutenant at the OSS training school when he was shown an ink-
blot and asked to describe what he saw. He stared at it conscientiously
for several minutes and said: "It's an inkblot." He was rejected for
overseas duty as uncooperative and anti-social.

What does it take to recover the pristine sense of an image?
Plato said that if we died for a time and came back to life, the most
ordinary things and actions would seem miraculous. Thornton
Wilder may have acted on Plato's suggestion in *Our Town,* when he
gave us an empty stage and forced us to imagine a kitchen and a
variety of places and things. Later, when the dead woman returned
to her former home for a single day and saw everything from the
perspective of death, we shared her vision. I can still see the imaginary
breakfast being cooked on an imaginary stove as clearly now as the
night I saw the scene on stage, more than fifteen years ago.

Sometimes, the object itself dies and is resurrected by
the archeologist or the art historian, and the drama of its re-discovery
restores it to freshness. Then the museum renders us the service of
removing the precious object from its context of utility and enshrining
it in a glass case or on a pedestal.

So, we present the match-box label, removed from its
box and surrounded by many other similar labels. They were never
intended to be seen this way. Your native of a remote district in
India will never in his lifetime see the box of matches intended for
Ireland or the Argentine, unless through some miracle, he chances
upon this issue of PRINT.

We became fascinated by the imagery of the match-box
labels and wrote a letter to the Swedish Match Company in Stockholm.
"Who designed these labels?" I asked, "Who decided on the particular

image for each country, someone in the country in which the matches were to be sold, or a designer in your factory at Jonkoping? How do you explain the violence that flares up so frequently among the labels? We see tigers attacking horses, men fighting lions with their bare hands; natives crouching in ambush waiting to thrust a murderous spear; labels entitled THE KILL; other labels show men in battle, mythological monsters, volcanoes and warriors on frightened, rearing horses. Even the quiet pictures and scenes seem to be unquiet, brooding and surreal in an uncouth, and menacing way, and show us strange countries of the mind rather than the lands in which the matches will be sold. How can you explain. . . .?" I went on in this vein.

I received the answer I deserved. "We are sorry that we do not have the information you have requested. The designs were made about fifty years ago and except for some slight changes, remain in use today. The names of the designers and other such information is no longer available."

Now, thrown back on the necessity of making my own guesses, I have hit on the following:

That the flaring up of the match when it is struck evokes images associated with fire. The first of the images is the camp-fire in the jungle and the ring of darkness on the periphery of the clearing. In the darkness there are animals waiting for the fire to die out so that they can move in for the kill. Worse than the lion or tiger out there in the darkness is the fear that they might be there. Staring into the camp-fire itself brings out Rorschach-like images of monsters and men who wait in ambush ready to kill. And pretty girls.

The type of mythological images which appear so frequently on the labels are described in some psychoanalytical writing. H.G. Baynes, the English Jungian has something to say the meaning of fire in his *Mythology of The Soul:*

"Intense activity in the unconscious is frequently accompanied by disturbing abdominal or cardiac symptoms. The smoke and fire coming from the nostrils of pictured monsters represent this idea of intense inner activity. When vital energy is introverted into the depths of the unconscious, it is sometimes as though the subject were bathed in primordial fire.

"We find this idea of life through fire in the initiatory rituals of the Eleusinian mystery-cult. The initiate had to go through the heart of a furnace which seemed to him like imminent death. In Rider Haggard's SHE Ayesha regains immortal youth by plunging into a pillar of fire revolving in the heart of a mountain.

"The idea of seeking renewal of life in a volcano is also found among certain Melanesian tribes. According to Layard, who lived for a time on the island of Malekula, the idea of joining the ancestral spirits in the heart of an active volcano is the supreme desire of the natives of Atchin and Vao. They have no fear of being devoured by fire. Apart from this belief they also venerate a god-hero who lights up both sun and moon. This god, Tagar, belongs to another tradition and is concerned with creating light rather than fire."

Another idea that comes to mind in connection with the symbolism in the designs of the match-box labels is. . . .

My thoughts on this subject are interrupted by a sudden recollection of my young Lieutenant in the OSS who claimed that he saw only an ink-blot. Maybe there are many, many more like him than I ever suspected, and a match-box label is only a match-box label. . . .

CHRIST, ICONS, AND MASS MEDIA

by

Spencer C. Bennett

CHRIST, ICONS, AND MASS MEDIA

by

Spencer C. Bennett

In our new age of iconography we are strangely akin to the formality of Byzantine Christianity and the conceptions that go with it. The icons of those early days of faith were universal in implication, strong in outline but vague in the portrait of any one personality. Today the telephone, the television, and the automobile are the objective counterparts of the ancient icons of fruits, birds and animals, all symbolizing some aspect of Christian belief or the Gospels. Both ages are the same in that they provide us with images and roles but not with individuality. The icons of the saints left much to be desired in terms of character portrayal but they leave no doubt as to the role the saint played in the life of the church. James Bond, the Playgirl of the Month, Richard Nixon—all of these

emerge in our time, not as individual human beings, but as role players
and iconographical objects produced by media. In film—the seer of
our day—heroes are transformed by the excitement the medium itself
engenders. In Antonioni's *Blow Up,* for example, the high point of
the film has nothing to do with the personal life of the hero. It
comes, instead, when we participate in the experience of his profession
photography. As the hero blows up a particular shot of shrubbery
until a body appears and murder is evident, we too are involved in
the process and it is the idea of the medium of film as its content
which leaves us fascinated.

Anonymity, however, bothers us. The more our identity
is related to roles, the less we think of ourselves as persons. Madison
Avenue has seen this and attempts to give us an identity through the
individualization of our objects. No man thinks of his Ford Mustang
as the copy of a million others or of his split level ranch as anything
less than a Ponderosa. But we live in the illusion of nineteenth century
romanticism here. Our icons are copies of an archetype which make
us one in our reverence for them. A Campbell soup can is a Campbell
soup can is a Campbell soup can. Technology has produced a world
of tangible universals.

Our selfconsciousness about individuality is a fairly
recent development. Ancient and medieval man identified himself
through his work, and his work was his contribution to the community
The fact that the majority of art from the past is anonymous is well
known. The windows in Chartre are for the most part the gift of no
one donor. They are contributions from the various trades. In the
past one's role in the creation of a cathedral or in transcribing
Scriptures was one's identity. There was no search for the meaning
of man outside of vocation.

Since modern man believes that technology has robbed
him of the possibility to be creative in his work, he has sought his
identity outside of vocation. How is he to do this? Obviously the
role of consumer offers little creative challenge? What has resulted
is an existential caricature of man. Man now exists in a vacuum of
contingency with only his freedom and nowhere to go. Automation
has programmed us out of our former existence and has given us no

clues as to where to look for a new one.

At this point, the iconography of the past has much to
say to us. Neither anonymity nor the importance of roles are new
phenomena in history. Technology in and of itself is neutral if new.
And the attempt on the part of Western man to give himself definition
outside of his role as technological men is bizarre if not impossible.
There is nothing to discourage him and everything to encourage him
to find parallels between his own iconography and that of the past.

For one thing, the icons of the early Eastern Church
made little distinction between the offices of the secular and the
religious. The kingship of Christ was the model for an interpretation
of government. Unlike the Western Church, the East held that the
Emperor assumed the leadership of the Church in his office as well
as the authority of secular role. This merging of the secular and
sacred office takes on particular significance in the icons of coronations
where the depiction of the royal event defies any desire on the part
of modern man to read into them individual personalities, geographic
location and dates. They are meant to be universal events since the
concept behind them is not based on the usual distinctions between
sacred and profane event.

The usual separation of roles no longer holds in our
time either. Icons of John F. Kennedy hang on the walls of rooms
all over the world. If martydom is one side of the iconographical
role, certainly Kennedy's attempt to bridge the gap between religious
belief and secular action was another. No longer are the new clergy
vertically orientated. Harry Emerson Fosdick was replaced by Martin
Luther King. King was as openly a man of the cloth as Fosdick but
we who viewed the media never saw King in any other light than as
a symbol of the clash which comes when values held to be eternal
become particularized in history. The task of the Church is to become
the servant of the world and the doors between the sanctuary and
the street are no longer visible.

The time seems ripe for a reinterpretation of the meaning
of space and time as well, but this requires some explanation. The
ancient icons have a contemporary air about them because they do
away with the distinctions between sacred time and sacred space

and the temporal world. This was more true of Eastern Christianity
than of the Western Church. Western man viewed Christ's death
and resurrection as the promise of a total victory over the forces of
alienation in creation that would come with the *parousia* or final
appearance of Christ. There would be an interim of time in which
it would often seem as though the darker forces of civilization would
destroy the earth. So the early Western Christians felt themselves
partially bound by a linear concept of history. Consequently liturgy
and even art was based upon a consciousness of the Christian year.[1]

On the other hand, the eternal quality of Eastern icons
is due in part to the belief by the East that every service of worship
was a celebration of the total victory over death. Eastern Christians
believed that there was no psychic distance between themselves and
the departed saints. Nor was there any time lapse between the sacrifice
of Christ on the cross (emphasized in the West) and the victory over
alien powers on Easter Sunday. The result of the Passion Story for
the East was the immediate transformation of creation into a transecul.
medium revealing the power of God's glory. And the regal formality
of the icons at St. Sophia are in every way representative of this spirit
of at-one-ness in space and time.

If the message of Eastern Christianity is shrouded in
mystery for contemporary man, the concept of a universal time is
not. The distance between psychological time and external measure-
ment of time may still hold although film is quickly erasing these
catagories.[2] But there is no doubt that we have passed beyond a
relative sense of time to a sense that all time distinctions are artificial.
What time is it in outer space? How much time do we have before
the bomb is dropped? How far away from Viet Nam are we in
seconds via satellite? When we say we have no time for ourselves
we are correct. To paraphrase Rudy Vallee, "My time is your time
when Walter Cronkite is on the screen." Like the concept of individua.
outside of role, the meaning of personal time is hard to come by in a
technological era.

What about space? The icons are not interested in that
dimension except as the simple locale of contact between God and
man. No particular place was sacred since the cross and Easter meant

the reconsecration of all space. Space is merely the place of event.
Today we can grasp the framework if not the content of this idea.
Media have erased the old notions of space. Immediate presence is
a consequence of T.V. (and the lack of dimension bother us no less
than it did the early Christians as they viewed the icons). It is an
interesting phenomenon that in the film *2001* the viewer's traditional
concepts of space have been so exhausted by the end of the film
that the director felt himself under compulsion to represent huge
distances as color and light rather than as depth and height. Our old
categories of space and time no longer hold.

  It must be made clear that the parallel I am making is
between the iconographical format of a former era and our own. It
remains to be seen whether anything can be salvaged from the specific
content of Christianity. The icon did not originate with Christianity.
It was a cultural formula used by most of the mystery religions. What
the icons of our day have in common with those of the past is an
emphasis on human roles versus the notion of man as an existential
creature and a dissolution of the categories of space and time. The
differences between the two ages are obvious as well. The content
of the early icons had to do with the mythology of religion as a
transecular medium while our icons of technology have to do with
the myths of empiricism.

  Nevertheless, although our media are results of an
empirical science, they have put man back in the corner of meta-
physics. Mass production is based upon a psuedo-Platonic schema
of models and forms from which reality is constructed. Sensitivity
training is only one of a number of transempirical interpretations
suggesting that human fulfillment is not limited to the senses,
although it can be expressed in no other way.

  The rise of the drug cults, the recent boom in astrology
and the fascination with psychedelia are all testimonials to our desire
to reach out beyond the senses without losing what they have to
offer. To add to the confusion I would attempt a reinterpretation
of an ancient icon—a Christian one in which the sight of the secular
is not lost. It is Jesus in the role the Church assigned him as the
miracle worker or exorciser of evil spirits.[3] It is the one aspect of

his life which has been most neglected by contemporary theology because it has seemed so incompatible with the selfunderstanding of modern man.[4] Yet, there are many things in this image of Jesus which are extremely relevant. For one thing, it represents the most tangible aspect of Jesus' ministry since it puts him in the role of miracle worker where visible demonstration is necessary. But for another, it lends itself to psychological analysis. The result of Jesus' healing is always a restoration of the human spirit as well as the making whole of the body. Part of the cure is the re-establishment of the patient in the life of the community.

Of course, the healings themselves are problematic in terms of our experience of the empirical world as a closed system of possibilities. But as metaphors, they lend themselves to the modern mind set. Our own technology has given rise to an acceptance of a fantasy world. Commercials where objects dance and sing, TV program where humans fly or escape permanent brain damage from blows that would kill ordinary men—these are all a part of our mythology. We don't accept these events as literal reality and yet we all pattern our lives on the kind of vicarious experience they offer. The distance between reality and fantasy, between disbelief on the basis of logic and belief on the basis of desire is a common theme of our stage and screen as well as the Gospels.

The kind of archetype which Jesus as the exorciser provides for use of modern media is also compatible with the iconographic outline. The miracles necessitate no historical context nor do they demand a fuller picture of Jesus as a personality other than giving us a picture of his magical role. They are a perfect instance of the merging of sacred and profane event and the shattering of our usual notions of time as process. Yet the result of the healings ties in with the necessity for living in communion with each other.

In addition, the picture of Jesus as a healer helps to bridge the gap which has existed between the life of the Church and the life of the secular world. Here is the one instance in the New Testament where Jesus reveals his authority to the secular world as the healer of broken human spirits. All of the Gospels find this in contradistinction to much of the tradition surrounding him which had to do with the intradisciplinary life of the Church. Any Hellenistic reader of the New Testament would have recognized the Jesus of the miracles since such magicians were a part of his cultural environment. It is the Christ who speaks in cryptic language in the New Testament about the future tribulations of the Church and his own hidden identity that would have puzzled a Greek reader.

In our time a new appreciation of the restorative power at work in our culture is revolutionizing the theological enterprise. Those areas of American life which have been transformed emotionally into new attitudes have not been those traditionally associated with the life of the Church. The civil rights movement, the crusade against the war in Viet Nam, and the new morality are suspect by many in the Church as being anti-Christian. But for others it is in these areas that Christianity, if not by name, is mainly at work. The new respect for the quality of human life evidenced by many of the protest groups is in keeping with the Christian concept of the incarnation. Furthermore a great deal of the new philosophy being formulated on the basis of this more positive attitude seems to find its expression through popular culture. Like the miracles for first Century Man, popular culture as the medium for our day has a direct appeal on the basis of recognized cultural patterns.

These parallels invite commentary on those iconoclastic tendencies in our culture which approximate the spirit which Jesus as the exorciser represented for the early Christians. One of the groups which is most in line with this analysis is the Beatles. First their format is that of anonymity and role playing. Although this group is comprised of multitalented individuals, nobody thinks of them as anything less than a unity. Their anonymity is purposeful and deliberate They cultivate their ability to assume many roles but they never do so at the expense of fragmentizing that strong outline of the four of them in any one song or film. It's Sargent Pepper's Lonely Heart's Club Band but Sargent Pepper is a corporate entity.

They also deal with time and space in terms of their universal implications. Time is important as a medium through which transtemporality can be expressed. The same is true of space. In a

Ravi Shankar arrangement called "Within You, Without You,"
they sing:

> We were talking—about the space
> between us all
> And the People—who hide themselves
> behind a wall of illusion
> Never glimpse the truth—then its far
> too late—when they pass away.[5]

The Beatles are concerned with age, human improvement and death.
Although they are not above a thrust at human foibles such as greed
("Piggies") and immature idealism ("Revolution I") they are for
the most part optimists about the possibilities of human nature.
            Even more in the iconographical mold is the fact that
all of their songs are relevant to the aura of our cultural patterns
but none of them can be pinned down to specific event. They depend
on electronic media but they do not manipulate them without allowing
them first to suggest aural possibilities. Thematically they deal in
mythology and parable rather than allegory. Rolewise, they assume
the position of the exorciser more than any other. They attempt to
speak to alienation and move the listener or the subject from the
position of self-containment into community. For all of their
eccentricities, the Beatles have a social view of man. The symphonic
form of *Sargent Pepper's Lonely Heart's Club Band* centers on the
movement into and out of common communion.

> You're such a lovely audience,
> We'd like to take you home with us,
> We'd love to take you home.[6]

And if some kind of eschatology is suggested by *Magical Mystery
Tour*, it is not a trip you take by yourself, but only through the
experience of the group.

> I've got an invitation

> To make a reservation
> The Magical Mystery Tour is waiting
>   to take you away
> Waiting to take you away.[7]

The magical side of the Beatles and their view of themselves as exorcisers of evil spirits in the community becomes especially clear in the film *The Yellow Submarine*. Besides creating a revolution in the format of the cartoon, the film dwells upon some very real forms of human alienation. The lonely sterility of Elleanor Rigby, the hollow shell of intellectual activity which comprises the life of the Nowhere Man, and the threat of the Meanies who attain metaphorical status by draining the color and sound out of life—all of these comprise a Beatle-like statement about human isolation and its consequences. In the film the Beatles represent a rejuvenating force. They are the Four Horsemen of the Apocalypse in a submarine. Sargent Pepper's music has restorative powers in a world that has lost its zest for life. The band explores the sense of celebration through fantasy without attempting to paraphrase the soap opera atmosphere of Walt Disney. And because the Beatles depend as much on the innovative use of the cartoon as a medium as they do upon their music to convey the need for communical celebration, they emerge as magicians who use illusion to tell us something very true about ourselves.

There are other iconoclastic figures in the movies. *Alice's Restaurant* admits (if somewhat begrudgingly) of the possibility that magicians of the soul exist. Ray and Alice Brock appear as larger- than- life figures in this film as they reconsecrate a church to the celebration of life without regard to secular and religious distinctions. Around them bands a community of faith who deem it no less appropriate to sing "Where Have All the Flowers Gone?" than "Amazing Grace" (or maybe its the other way around) at a Thanksgiving feast. *Alice's Restaurant* is a place for recovery and healing of psyche and body as well.

It is true that *Alice's Restaurant* has trouble containing the figures of Alice and Ray. As a symbol Alice assumes the pro-

portions of mother earth or of a fertility goddess and Ray the ex-
travagance of personified grace. The director obviously had trouble
reconciling this universal aspect of their characters with the subplot
of their individual relationship. So the film is ambiguous and
especially the ending where Alice outlined against the church evokes
a Mona Lisa wistfulness and moment of doubt in the viewer's consciousness. But the more cosmic dimensions of the film focus on
those moments when the community comes together for a holiday,
a wedding or a funeral and the health of communion is apparent.
Who could doubt that it is Alice and Ray that provide the useful
archetypes for the structuring of these moments of universal joy
and sorrow? They seem to be the source of motion so necessary
to the message of the film.

    Cool Hand Luke is another film which revolves around
the kind of secular magic which restores humanity. This time Paul
Newman as the hero through the defiance of the guards and the
performance of Olympian feats (such as eating fifty eggs in an hour)
transforms the lives of the inmates of a Southern prison farm.
Through his acts the prisoners realize their own potential for creativity
even under stifling conditions. Thus a work crew finishes a day's
work of paving in half the time for the sheer excitement of the
possibility of such a task.

    Another figure even more classic in design than Cool
Hand Luke is McMurphy in Ken Kesey's *One Flew Over The Cuckoo's
Nest.* A novel of great theological significance, this book centers on
the activity of a huge Irishman who enters a mental asylum and im-
mediately notes that the disorders of inmates are more the result of
present fear than of past traumas. McMurphy brings confidence to
the ward by achieving a superhuman dimension in which he is able
to overcome all obstacles the institution and its personification in
"Big Nurse" put in his way. When McMurphy can't brush his teeth
because the toothpaste is locked up, he uses cleanser as a substitute.
When there is no mix for the alcohol at a mutinous party in the ward
McMurphy resorts to cough syrup. As the inmates become human
again through McMurphy's mirthful exploits the books takes on intended aspects of the Passion Story. But basically the book's theme

is the possibility of the transformation of existence.

What is important in the four examples given above is not the individual portrait of the heroes but rather the effect they have on the understanding of community. The Beatles, Cool Hand Luke, Alice and Ray Brock, and McMurphy are roles. Whether they exist or not is irrelevant as long as their invention has served the purpose. They have been molded as exorcisers of society by media just as Jesus was given stature by the early Church as healer in iconographical form. Nor do time and space matter in the cosmological dimension of the art. In the Thanksgiving scene of *Alice's Restaurant* the camera pans for a long shot of the festival to give us the impression that all space is contained in this moment of joy. In *One Flew Over The Cuckoo's Nest* when McMurphy finally does battle with Big Nurse, it is an eschatological event outside of history.

The emphasis is on the transtemporal content of the icon. Both modern and ancient icons were and are objects of veneration. But they are venerated because they share in the reality of the concept behind them by association. There is nothing about the objectivity of an icon in and of itself which commands our attention. Like illusions, icons are springboards for perceptions. The best analogy to the iconographical concept is in contemporary theatre where we are just beginning to realize the value of illusion for the perception of deeper values. Did George and Martha actually have a child in *Who's Afraid of Virginia Woolf?* It makes no difference. What does make a difference is that George and Martha go beyond their games in the last act to see each other as persons. Media aid understanding because it is media through which we see something else. And again that is a feature of icons. But media is also iconographical—especially electronic media—in that it reduces all time and space to one image, literally,   in the case of TV, to one channel. Far from erecting conceptual barriers between the icons of our time and those of the first three centuries of Christianity, media make it possible for us to share common images.

NOTES

[1]Chapter III in Yngve Brilioth's *Eucharistic Faith and Practice* is especially helpful in pointing out the differences in the worship of the East

West. Translated by A.G. Hebert, (London   SPCK, 1961), pp. 71-78.

[2]As movie goers become more sophisticated, they have less desire to distinguish between fantasy and reality in the film. Fellini's *Juliet of the Spirits* remains all one piece regardless of the constant switches from Julie's inner world to the outer world.

[3]So much of the Gospels is composed of these miracles stories that it is impossible to go very deeply into New Testament criticism without meeting them. For example the fifth chapter of Mark is nothing but three of these stories strung together.

[4]Yet, there are few New Testament scholars in the liberal vein who do not find these miracle stories to be an embarrassment in the presentation of the Gospel to the empirical mind of modern man. (See Rudolf Bultmann's "demythologizing" argument in *Kerygma and Myth,* ed. H.W. Bartsch, vol i-ii, 1962). While I sympathise with the problem as a purely theological one, I think this image of Jesus as a miracle worker has value as a metaphorical bridge between the Gospel and contemporary popular culture.

[5]*Sargent Pepper's Lonely Hearts Club Band,* Capitol Records, SMAS 2653.

[6]*Ibid.*

[7]*Magical Mystery Tour,* Capitol Records, 2835.

ARTIFACTS: FOLK, POPULAR,
IMAGINARY AND REAL

by

Henry Glassie

ARTIFACTS: FOLK, POPULAR,
IMAGINARY AND REAL*

by

Henry Glassie

In the shaggy light of a space set aside for the purpose,
a man has hammered at metal, hacked at wood, and joined the
materials into an artifact. It is April, 1969, and the United States.
Possibly the space is a studio, the artifact sculpture, the man an
artist. If so, chances are he has bent his back and brain to the task
of novelty, struggling to make a thing that has never been made
before, hoping for the attention of the cognoscenti. With luck he
will have a series of exclusive shows; he will become famous and
rich; Sandak will publish a slide of his thing. The space could be a
suburban basement, the artifact an adjustable, colonial lamp-bookcase-
bar, the man an ulcer-plagued insurance salesman. No less than the
artist, perhaps, he is sensitive to the materials and he takes joy out

of the act of making, but his effort has been to relax, to reproduce
in three dimensions an object detailed in two in the pages of a slick
magazine for modern homeowners. Or, the man might be lean and
aged Shannon York, open and bony in blue bib overalls, the space
his asbestos sided shop out near Moss, Tennessee, and the artifact a
corn knife, made because he likes "shop work" and a neighbor needs
something to chop the fodder on his hill farm. His drive is the replicatio
of the proved implement that he has been making all his life and that
his uncle, from whom the craft came, cranked out for the duration
of his.

A cacophony of American media publicly express a
national consistency--a covertly agreed upon set of (not necessarily
observed) ends and means--a mass norm--the ideal contour of the
culture presented daily in the paper, nightly on television, weekly
in the magazines, and definitively in the address with which Everett
McKinley Dirksen kicked off the Republican Convention of 1968. The
norm--American popular culture--is supported by an efficient syn-
chronization of economic, religious, and governmental power into
what Chief Broom in Ken Kesey's *One Flew Over the Cuckoo's Nest*
called the Combine. Material manifestations of this popular--normative-
culture line our walls, our highways, rip into our skies, transform and
become our land--our clothing, shelter, food. Simultaneously, things
are made which are incompatible with the norm, which differ from it
in one way or another, which are difficult or impossible to rationalize
as part of, what they are calling around the academic league nowadays,
the *Zeitgeist*. Some things may be seen as progressive with regard to
the public culture--things like the paintings Wassily Kandinsky made
after he found that one upside-down on his easel in 1908, or the
clocks John Fromanteel made in England after his visit to Holland
in 1657. The progressive deviation from the norm--labeled imperfectly
the elite or academic strain in culture--may gain esoteric patronage
and become sooner or later the norm. The mirror image of the
progressive in culture is the conservative. Just as at anytime there are
popular and elite artifacts, there are folk artifacts, such as Shannon
York's corn knife or the pipes for pot smoking which are fashioned
out of a toilet tissue tube and tin foil. Synchronically, the folk--con-

servative–thing is like the elite thing: it is not part of the national norm; rather it exists because of individual, group, or local acceptance. Diachronically, though, the elite and popular are similar, exhibiting great change across time, where the essence of a folk idea is its continuity with little change through time. The nearly static feeling that an array of folk things presents to the scholar, however, does not mean that folk cultures are not in constant flux, nor that folk things are nonfunctioning survivals: they are culture's constants exactly because of their basic utility.

The division of culture into three parts is defensible only as a matter of scholastic convenience. The isolation and study of only the folk, the popular, or the elite in culture is not defensible. Culture is broken down not to isolate that which is worth study but to prevent the elision of relevant information. In his wonderful paper delivered at the 1970 meeting of the Society for Historical Archaeology, Bernard L. Fontana emphasized the need for schemes for dividing and subdividing cultures and their products in artifactual interpretation–iconography in the terms of Marshall Fishwick's introduction to the book you are reading. The idea at the base of the division into progressive, normative, and conservative–elite, popular, and folk–may be of assistance to scholars in their task of bringing order into the phenomenal culture chaos they encounter (or should be encountering) constantly. The three words do not refer to entire societies or cultures (and they have nothing to communicate about economic level); their value comes during the process of breaking culture and its manifestations down for scrutiny. The mind of every man is apt to include ideas which can be classed as elite, popular, and folk: at least there is no one in America who does not carry both folk and popular culture. And, as the mind is a compound of ideas from various sources, the objects we can touch may be purely of one category, or they may represent syntheses–often, very complicated syntheses. The methods of those who study culture must be accordingly synthetic: a discipline draws the bits it wishes to study out of reality and arranges these into a scholastic construct; an interdisciplinary approach (as they call those timid mergers of, say, social history and literary history) draws out more bits, but its results are similarly skewed; the scholar needs to face-off with reality and

study it not from the comfort of some discipline, but seriously: if he
has not worried as James Agee worries in the initial movements of
Let Us Now Praise Famous Men, then his findings should be suspect.

There are folk traditions which spin deeply back through
time with no apparent influence from what some simplistically (and
ethnocentrically) refer to as "higher levels of culture." But, while
there are dying twitches of concern for folk purity, most folklorists
have become accustomed to discovering a Grub Street hack at the
source of today's folk ballad and a line of transmission patched with
broadsides and wax. In the same way, the folk ideas from which folk
artifacts flow through manual action have been constantly influenced
by popular culture.

The most usual result of the influence of popular on folk
material during the past 130 years in America, and particularly the
past fifty, has been the replacement of the traditional object by its
popular equivalent. The popular object has been accepted by the
innovative individual because it saves him time, is more quickly produced
or bought, and is easier to use than the traditional object–and also
because it is new. Slick salesmen and the numerous publications and
officials of both the government and private agencies are persistent
in recommending nontraditional material (which by no means always
represents an improvement) to individuals and groups which maintain
some orientation to tradition.[1] The recognized leaders of such groups
will often embrace the up-to-date to reinforce their status. The
members of a group which has a weak orientation to tradition tend
to follow the leader, with the individuals having the highest proportion
of folk elements in their culture being last in line.[2] The more traditionall
oriented groups may be split by progress: the innovative leader is not
completely followed because of the existence of (perhaps new) leaders
who are supported by a conservative anti-progress norm; the varieties
of Amish and Mennonite clothes and vehicles stand as material testimony
to the schisms produced in traditional communities by change stimulated
from without.[3] The replacement of folk by popular practice through
this incomplete and frequently prestige-stimulated acculturative process,
results, on the one hand, with the diminishing of tradition, but, on
the other, with the establishment of the folk nature of certain aspects

of behavior which may have been previously popular and before that elite. In the late 1860's and early 1870's, the writers in the agricultural periodicals, which were committed to "improvement," recommended the use of various patent metal spiles, the short tubes used to conduct the sap from the hole drilled in the maple tree into the bucket. These were quickly adopted by maple syrup and sugar producers. And the plastic tubes recently introduced to replace the metal spile have also been widely accepted. But a few small producers continue to make and use wooden spiles of the type which has been in use since the mid-eighteenth century; the wooden spile is surely folk and has been for about a century.[4]

Popular culture's agents frequently apply extensive and unpleasant pressure to conservative individuals or groups in an attempt to bring them into line with "modern thinking"; the pattern of the popular culture, that is. Clashes between cultures which are different and independently valid can be especially tragic when one of the cultures is able to mobilize the kind of vast power that the American national norm can, for then the weaker culture is likely to be cast as a twisted, degenerate version of the dominant culture. The theme of the Department of Labor publication called "The Moynihan Report" is that the traditional black family is a disintegrated version of the small, patrifocal middle class American family,[5] although the publication goes on to prove implicitly that the structureless family it is attacking has a structure–it is just a different structure. The sort of culturally naive ethnocentricism which frames *The Negro Family: The Case for National Action* is particularly horrifying when frozen (as it is now) into policy.[6]

The impetus of popular culture is usually sufficient to engender desired changes, and only rarely has it been felt necessary to legislate against folk tradition. Building codes, however, occasionally prevent the construction or maintenance of folk housing;[7] many traditional hunting and fishing techniques have been outlawed;[8] and homemade corn liquor remains "blockade," "bootleg," "moonshine" –illegal.[9] The laws against it restrict the extent to which it is produced, but the distillation of corn persists. It persists because it is economical: it is less expensive than "bonded liquor," being untaxed, and it can be made and sold for good profit with a small capital outlay; accordingly

it is common in areas where income is low. It persists in dry country
because there any kind of whiskey is supposed to be hard to find.
But moonshine is not to be found in many areas where the economic
situation might suggest its presence. This is because its persistence
is due primarily to the fact that, in the Upland South particularly
(the steep country from which corn could be shipped more economically
in fruit jars than in bushel baskets), its technology, marketing, flavor,
and the morality which allow it to exist are traditional: moonshining
goes back through the eighteenth century in America and to an earlier
time in Ireland.[10] In many sections of the South corn liquor is preferred
to bottled-in-bond, and flavored with bubble gum (as at least one
black man from the Carolina Sea Islands makes it) or with a peppermint
stick dissolved into it (as it often is along the Blue Ridge), or mixed
half and half with water and a large spoonful of sugar (the way the
mountain farmer drinks it), it can be a fine drink.

The absorption of alien traditions and the synthesis of
foreign and familiar traditions can be facilitated by the recognition
on the part of a builder of the similarities shared by things which are
new and old to him. Externally viewed, it seems that when similar
material exists at the same time in the inventories of adjacent cultures
and in the mind of an individual, a mutual or one-sided movement of
influence results in the increased similarity of the two traditions.
By the end of the last century, the banjo, which has clear African
antecedents,[11] had been developed into two five-string forms. One
was the popular, factory-produced banjo, with its minstrel show and
college music club heritage, which had a pearly, fretted fingerboard,
Italianate decoration, and a large head held taut by mechanical brackets.
The other had no frets and a head only about six inches in diameter
which was stretched over a light wooden or tin rim forced gently into
a thicker wooden rim (Fig. 1). This second, folk, type was found in
the Southern Mountains; its strings were catgut and its head was
groundhog, cat, or squirrel skin: "The one I learned on, my brother
made it, a homemade banja. Killed a cat, tanned its hide, made the
head, and he carved out the rest of it. And then he bought one."[12]
Most contemporary Southern Mountain banjo pickers play "store-
boughten" instruments, but in northwestern North Carolina and

adjacent southwestern Virginia there are still several men who make banjoes of the old type, not because they cannot afford or are unaware of factory products, but because they prefer a fretless instrument: "I would not take fifty bracket banjers for one good fretless."[13] These modern fretless banjoes are held together with screws, strung with metal strings, and the heads are regularly ordered from a musical supply house; otherwise they are essentially the same as those in use sixty and more years ago. Within the past decade the banjo builders have experimented with instruments which look more like the "northern" or "bracket" banjoes: occasionally they are built with frets or with a head that is larger than usual (Fig. 1 C), on most the peghead is contoured like a mass-produced banjo (Fig. 1 B), and very recently homemade imitations of expensive instruments like those seen on television and at country music parks, complete with mechanical pegs and brackets, have been produced (Fig. 1 D).

The interaction of popular and folk cultures has not resulted exclusively in modifications of folk culture–the vitality of today's best popular music comes directly (as in the case of the Chambers Brothers or Johnny Cash) or indirectly (as in the case of Bob Dylan or Jerry Garcia of the Grateful Dead) out of folk music. Material folk traditions, such as the regional and ethnic cookery made available in restaurants, festivals, bazaars, and especially cookbooks, have also been absorbed by the popular culture.[14]

Popular material objects may be based on borrowed folk models, and a folk tradition may, in turn, derive from a popular model. The first English settlers in the New World, of course, brought with them no tools designed specifically for chopping cornstalks. In the South, corn knives based on the machetes used to cut sugar cane and the similar knives of butchers came into use (Fig. 2A); a Virginia correspondent to *The American Farmer* in 1819 wrote: "Many farmers cut their corn with hoes. . . . The better course is to use knives, made in the form of a butcher's cleaver. They may be made of old straw knives, the blade about ten, and the shank and handles fifteen inches long."[15] In the Northeast, a distinctive corn knife type (Fig. 2 B-E) was devised, probably out of the ancient sickle-scythe tradition,[16] for, in those areas in which the L-shaped corn knife was used, some preferred to cut their corn with a grass hook or sickle.[17] To fill or create a demand for a commercially produced corn knife during the mid-nineteenth century, the popular manufacturers began turning out, and selling for about half a dollar, corn knives which were reproductions of the traditional northern and southern implements.[18] The preeminence of Yankee factories seems to have led to the spread of the northern corn knife form, so that since about 1880 many of the corn knives made in the South have been patterned after the northern ones (Fig. 1 F—G The northern and southern corn knives of the early 1880's were folk products; the corn knives of the nineteenth century factories were popular imitations of folk originals; the homemade northern corn knife of the late nineteenth century is a folk product reinforced by popular acceptance; the modern southern corn knife is a folk imitation of a popular model.

The folklorist cringes when an untruth is passed off as "just folklore"; the serious student of material culture is equally anguished by the way the term "folk art" is popularly used. In both cases "folk" has been qualitatively interpreted to mean that which is substandard: folklore to some historians is bad information; "folk art" to some art historians is bad art. The usual statement on "folk art" takes into account only two kinds of American art--academic and "folk."[19] Most of the antiquarians who employ the term do worry about their use of it and they have proposed a number of alternatives--naive, provincial, unselfconscious, primitive, anonymous, and nonacademic (this last being perhaps the only term which can happily encompass the hodgepodge of objects normally displayed in "folk art" galleries).[20] The distinctions made in this essay between folk and popular cultures can be used as a guide to "folk art." Most of "folk art" is not folk because it is popular; the paintings made on velvet by young ladies in the seminaries and academies, for example.[21] Another big piece of "folk art" is not folk because, although it does not reflect a national norm, it is not traditional; such would be the daublings of untutored geniuses.[22] A problem perhaps harder to attack is determining how much of the material which is genuinely folk, is art. Art is the application of an aesthetic, so that it can include more than paintings and sculpture; listen to this democratic voice from the New Deal days:

We now recognize that the aesthetic
experience can be as deep and as genuine
to the one who uses soil, or wood, or
grass to shape his best concept as to
one who does the same with paint and
marble; and that the spade, the ax, and
the scythe are as much tools for artistic
expression as are the brush and the
chisel.[23]

In all things that man makes there is an aesthetic factor;
there is no artifact totally devoid of art.[24] It is often only the aesthetic
nature of an object which the foreign viewer can appreciate, but
most objects are the result of complex intentions and frequently they
function simultaneously in different systems in the culture; the New
Mexican *santo* is sculpture to the collector; to the maker it was sculpture
but it was also a material manifestation of a deep faith and was therefore
not only decoration, but as well a tool in the maintenance of mental
and social health.[25] Depending upon his training or taste, the scholar
often places all of his emphasis on one of an artifact's several properties,
although ideally the scholar would comprehend the balance between
the artistic and the practical aspects of an object. Useful toward this
end is the concept offered by George Kubler of an aesthetic to practical
continuum, with the antagonistic corollaries that there is a distinction
between art and craft, and that all things are a mixture of the aesthetic
and the practical.[26]

Although often treated as art, most folk material is only
secondarily aesthetic in intent and function; it is craft. Decoys bring
good prices at antique shows and are exhibited in galleries of art,
but they existed mainly to lure birds within shotgun range. In
some instances the craftsman transcended necessity and carved and
painted a decoy which pleased him; most of the time, though, the
decoy was designed to please only the ducks (Fig. 3). The decoy
brought pleasure to the maker possibly, and it had to be appealing to
the buyer-hunter, but it was stored in a pile in a shed, tossed in icy
waters and shot up; the aesthetics of the decoy are real but submerged--

mostly, it must ride right on the water and be of a shape and coloration which will bring ducks to the blind, money to the wallet. Recently som traditional makers of decoys, like Lem Ward of Crisfield, Maryland, have taken the pains to produce folk sculpture for the collector's shelf instead of stool to float in the gunner's rig.[27] But in the United States there has been little painting or sculpture produced primarily as the fulfillment of a folk aesthetic,[28] and the one area of material folk culture which can parallel much of oral tradition in that it thrives and is produced and maintained more for aesthetic than practical reasons is exterior decoration. The geometric painting on barns found not only in Pennsylvania, but in Ohio and Virginia too,[29] and the neat islands of bright perennial flowers bordered by whitewashed rocks or tractor tires found in front yards through much of the countryside are among America's grandest folk artistic traditions.

There is no reason why the diverse things found in a "folk art" gallery should not be displayed together on curatorial whim, but those things cannot be interpreted properly without knowing which are art and to which the adjective "folk" is appropriate. There is nothing in an artifact which would indicate whether it is folk or not— "folk" is not a "style," though the word is often treated in that way; rather, there are many styles from Yankee Coast Severe to New Mexico Adobe Baroque to Pastel Ghetto Dingy to Time Lag Great Lakes Greek Revival which can be folk. And, the critic's consideration of an object as art does not mean that it was intended as art; his aesthetic evaluation of a thing which is a product of cultural laws of taste which he does not understand is merely Victorian silliness. To make accurate distinctions the scholar needs information on the artifact's context—at the very least he must know its use and its provenance in time and space. Artifacts lacking this kind of data may have monetary worth as antiques; they are often pictured in books and exhibited in museums; but they are as worthless to the serious student of material culture as a dusty, unidentified fragment of a cranium is to the physical anthropologist.

With sufficient information, the artifact becomes worth study. Studying it shatters it, for as Paul Klee commented, the forms we see in nature and art are combinations and to comprehend them, "we must dissect them to reveal their component parts."[30] Dissected, the artifact becomes understandable: its parts, past, and associations become traceable: the artifact can be viewed as the product and source of meaning. The assignation of meaning to a thing brings it value in the same way to the people who make and use it and to the people who study it. A thing is only a thing until a man wanders into the picture and begins relating the thing to other things; then, the thing becomes an icon. (This is not just a thing, it is a stonewall; it is not just a stonewall, it is an English type of stonewall built in Massachusetts: it is a symbol of the cultural ancestry of New England, of cooperation, of ownership, of man's relation with the land. . . .) The conceptualization of associations, relations, and meaning is the recognition of the thing's functions and of the icon's power.

Before it is made the artifact is a linkage of ideas–a plan for the object's physical being–and it is a projected icon: it will function serving multiple (intentional and unintentional, obvious and obscure) purposes in the culture. Once it is in existence it will be a source for makers of other things and it will influence the behavior of those who use it. As it continues to live, either as a physical entity or a mental image, its significance may change, just as the literary interpretations of a great novel shift with the times. A cabin built out of logs in a far mountain cove was designed to function in both the economic and aesthetic systems of the culture—it was built that way because it looked right, had a handy amount of space and comfortable interior volumes; it was built that way because a young couple wanted to go out on their own,[31] and, given the restrictive tradition, well, what other house could you build? When everyone else began building of frame, this log cabin, then a little old, was a source of shame, but now it has become a symbol for many of the good life left behind when they moved to the city; "the little old log cabin in the mountains" has been used regularly for the past three decades in country and western music as a metaphor for the simple, clean, Christian life abandoned for bleak, unfriendly Detroit Town. People foreign to the culture of the maker of the artifact also use it in symbolic ways. To continue with the example of the mountain cabin, people with programs on their mind have used it to stand for the totality of

Appalachian poverty--thirteen children crowded into a one room house; wind whining through the slits between the logs from which the chinking has fallen--books as separated by time as *The Church's Mission to the Mountaineers of the South*[32] and *Night Comes to the Cumberlands: A Biography of a Depressed Area*[33]begin visually with photographs of log cabins. The cabin which stimulates pity in those contexts may be seen by the historian as a symbol of the syncretism of British and Germanic cultures on the Appalachian frontier, and by the cultural geographer as a symbol for a section of the landscape.[34]

The ideas activated in the making of artifacts are constantly drawn from a great variety of sources, so that part of a thing may be old and part of it new. The ideas held about objects can influence each other in the same manner. Symbolism developed externally can be assimilated; the result is selfconsciousness in folk culture and works of art like Andy Adams' *The Log of a Cowboy*[35] and Lou Rawls' "Southside Blues."[36] The watermen who dredge oysters off the bottom of the Chesapeake Bay from the slippery decks of V-bottom sloops, called batteaus, drudge boats, or skipjacks,[37] have been told again and again that they work in the last sailing fishing fleet in North America--that they are the last of a brawny and bold, hearty race of men. No one has built a skipjack for fifteen years, but if, as Captain Junior Benton of Wenona, Maryland, predicted, skipjacks are built in the future (the work is hard but there is money in it), the process of production will contain a symbolic tone which was not present when Captain Benton's boat, the *Geneva May*, was built back in 1901. The maker of the new skipjack will be building a beautiful boat, a useful boat, and he-- like the *santero* in New Mexico, or the architect of the Temple of Concord at Agrigento--will be consciously producing a plastic metaphor.

While watching the builder of the new skipjack in the middle of the 1970's, while watching her ribs framed, the trailboards carved, the drudging equipment installed, it might occur to us that somewhere in a suburban basement an insurance man is running a plank (a plank that will become a leg of an adjustable, colonial. . .) through the screel and sawdust of his Christmas gift table saw; that in Frisco a furry chap is burning his mind out with meth and acid to clear away the cobwebs of culture so that the sculpture he is making can be new, new, new; that several thousand feet up a ledgy, velvet mountain in western North Carolina, a young man is whittling a fretless banjo neck out of a piece of walnut, just as his daddy and his grandaddy did before him. And we will be able to answer the question asked at the end of the introduction to this book. The answer is no.

NOTES

[*]This is an extensively revised version of pages 17 to 33 from *Pattern in the Material Folk Culture of the Eastern United States,* University of Pennsylvania Monographs in Folklore and Folklife, 1 (Philadelphia: University of Pennsylvania Press, 1969).

[1]For example: W.M. Williams, *The Country Craftsman* (London, 1958), p. 59.

[2]You should be referred here to B. Benvenuti, *Farming in Cultural Change* (Assen, 1962); Gwyn E. Jones, "The Nature and Consequences of Technical Change in Farming," *Folk Life,* 3 (1965), pp. 79-87; George M. Beal, "Decision Making in Social Change," in H. J. Schweitzer, *Rural Sociology in a Changing Urbanized Society* (Urbana, 1966), pp. 51-94.

[3]See, John Paul Yoder, "Social Isolation Devices in an Amish-Mennonite Community," unpublished master's thesis, Pennsylvania State College (1941); Calvin George Bachman, *The Old Order Amish of Lancaster Country* (Lancaster, 1961); John A. Hostetler, *Amish Society* (Baltimore, 1963).

[4]Darrell D. Henning, "Maple Sugaring: History of a Folk Technology," *Keystone Folklore Quarterly,* XI:4 (Winter, 1966), pp. 253-255.

[5]*The Negro Family: The Case for National Action* (Washington, 1965).

[6]See Conrad M. Arensberg and Solon T. Kimball, *Culture and Community* (New York, 1965), pp. 232-234.

[7]For example, Margaret Fay Shaw, *Folksongs and Folklore of South Uist* (London, 1955), p. 17.

[8]An excellent study with much on this subject is Edmund E. Lynch, "Fishing on Otsego Lake," unpublished master's thesis, Cooperstown Program, State University of New York (1965).

[9]Moonshine is one aspect of American material folk culture

which has interested people: Margaret W. Morley, *The Carolina Mountains* (Boston and New York, 1913), chapter XX; Horace Kephart, *Our Southern Highlanders* (New York, 1926), chapters V-XI; Charles Morrow Wilson, *Backwoods America* (Chapel Hill, 1934), chapter XIV; Thomas D. Clark, *The Kentucky* (New York and Toronto, 1942), chapter XXI; Charles S. Pendleton, "Illicit Whiskey-Making," *Tennessee Folklore Society Bulletin*, XII:1 (March, 1946), pp. 1-16; Muriel Earley Sheppard, *Cabins in the Laurel* (Chapel Hill, 1946), chaper XIII; Loyal Durand, Jr., " 'Mountain Moonshining' in East Tennessee," *The Geographical Review*, XLVI:2 (April, 1956), pp. 168-181; Leonard W. Roberts, *Up Cutshin and Down Greasy* (Lexington, 1959), chapter 4; Charles Morrow Wilson, *The Bodacious Ozarks* (New York, 1959), Chapter IV; Harry M. Caudill, *Night Comes to the Cumberlands* (Boston and Toronto, 1963), chapter 12; William Price Fox, "The Lost Art of Moonshine," *The Saturday Evening Post*, 239:7 (March 25, 1966), pp. 34-35; Cratis Williams, "Moonshining in in the Mountains," *North Carolina Folklore*, XV:1 (May, 1967), pp. 11-17; Tom Wolfe, *The Kandy-Kolored Tangerine-Flake Streamline Baby* (New York, 1969), pp 105-144.

[10]Kevin Danaher, *In Ireland Long Ago* (Cork, 1964), pp. 58-63.

[11]Gene Bluestein, "America's Folk Instrument: Notes on the Five-String Banjo," *Western Folklore*, XXIII:4 (October, 1964), pp. 241-248.

[12]Edgar A. Ashley, high school math teacher, banjo-picker, and tale-teller from Grassy Creek, Ashe County, North Carolina; tape-recorded interview, August 7,1962. *Märchen* learned from his father and told by Mr. Ashley can be found in *Tennessee Folklore Society Bulletin*, XXX: (September, 1964), pp. 97-102; *Mountain Life and Work*, XL: 2 (Summer, 1964), pp. 52-56.

[13]Mack Presnell, 67-year-old farmer, tale-teller, dulcimer and banjo player, from near Sugar Grove, Watauga County, North Carolina; interview June 16, 1963. Mr. Presnell would rather pick the banjo with his "magic finger" than work his small, steep farm. He would rather fish than pick the banjo.

[14]The number of regional and ethnic cookbooks is enormous; for representative examples of the kinds of books which have carried American folk cuisine into the popular kitchen see: Imogene Wolcott, *The Yankee Cook Book* (New York, 1939); Haydn S. Pearson, *The Countryman's Cookbook* (New York, and London, 1964); Ann Hark and Preston A. Barba, *Pennsylvania German Cookery* (Allentown, 1956); Mary Emma Showalter, *Mennonite Community Cookbook* (Philadelphia and Toronto, 1950); Mrs. B. C. Howard, *Fifty Years in a Maryland Kitchen* (New York, 1944); Marion Cabell Tyree, *Housekeeping in Old Virginia* (Louisville, 1890); Mary Ruth Chiles and Mrs. William P. Trotter, eds.,*Mountain Makin's in the Smokies* (Gatlinburg, 1957); Lessie Bowers, *Plantation Recipes* (New York, 1959); Mary Vereen Huguenin and Anne Montague Stoney, eds., *Charleston Receipts* (Charleston, 1966); Marjorie Kinnan Rawlings, *Cross Creek Cookery* (New York, 1942); Mary Land, *Louisiana Cookery* (Baton Rouge, 1954); Mary Faulk Koock, *The Texas Cookbook* (Boston and Toronto, 1965); Yeffe Kimball and Jean Anderson, *The Art of American Indian Cooking*

(Garden City, 1965); Jennie Grossinger, *The Art of Jewish Cooking* (New York, 1958); Theresa F. Bucchieri, *Feasting with Nonna Serafina* (South Brunswick, N.J., 1966); Josephine J. Dauzvardis, *Popular Lithuanian Recipes* (Chicago, 1955); Yasmine Betar, *Finest Recipes from the Middle East* (Washington, 1964); traditional Negro cookery has been featured in a "Soul Food" column in the monthly Sunday supplement *Tuesday*. Some of these cookbooks are surprisingly useful for the serious student of material culture.

[15]*The American Farmer*, I:38 (December 17, 1819), n. 306; see too, James Ringgold, "On the Best Mode of Harvesting Indian Corn," *The American Farmer*, IV:16 (July 5,1822), pp. 125-126.

[16]Axel Steensberg, *Ancient Harvesting Instruments: A Study in Archaeology and Human Geography* (Copenhagen, 1943), illustrates and describes in detail ancient and medieval angular sickles and short scythes very similar to the northern corn knife form. Possibly a sort of reverse evolution, cued by the thickness of the cornstalk, led from the balanced sickle to the corn knife.

[17]Charles S. Plumb, *Indian Corn Culture* (Chicago, 1895), pp. 102-103. See too, Neil Adams McNall, *An Agricultural History of the Genesee Valley, 1790-1860* (Philadelphia, 1952), p. 129.

[18]"Implements for Cutting Up Corn," *American Agriculturist*, XXVII:10 (October, 1868), p. 395. Both corn knife types are used in Pennsylvania; for examples: Russell S. Baver, "Corn Culture in Pennsylvania," *Pennsylvania Folklife*, 12:1 (Spring, 1961), p. 35: Kiehl and Christian Newswanger, *Amishland* (New York, 1954), p. 55. Both types are in use side by side in parts of the Upland South and Midwest; the type used, whether "chopping" (straight) or "cutting" (L-shaped), depends entirely on personal preference.

[19]For example, Nina Fletcher Little, *The Abby Aldrich Rockefeller Folk Art Collection* (Boston and Toronto, 1957), p. XIII.

[20]*Antiques*, LVII:5 (March,1950), includes "What is American Folk Art? A Symposium," pp. 355-362. The contributions are of varying worth. Jean Lipman's expresses the tired clichés best (or worst). The folklorist will be able to agree completely with none of them, but those which attempt to subdivide folk art are the most useful: that of E. P. Richardson (see also the introduction to his *A Short History of Painting in America* [New York, 1963]), that of James Thomas Flexner (you might also read his "The Cult of the Primitives," *American Heritage*, VI:2 [February, 1955], pp. 38-47), and that of Janet R. McFarlane and Louis C. Jones (see too: Agnes Halsey Jones and Louis C. Jones, *New-Found Folk Art of the Young Republic* [Cooperstown, 1960], pp. 7-9).

[21]These pictures are counted folk art in Holger Cahill, *American Folk Art: The Art of the Common Man in America 1750-1900* (New York, 1932), pp. 11, 18, plates 79-108. The great interest in "folk art" began with Cahill; since his time some advances in definition and treatment have been made; see,

William P. Campbell, *101 American Primitive Water Colors and Pastels from the Collection of Edgar William and Bernice Chrysler Garbisch* (Washington, 1966). In this book a careful distinction is made between Pennsylvania German *fraktur* which is folk art and the art of the nineteenth century school-girls which is not. Others, however, have made no progress toward a cultural understanding of "folk art"; for examples: Peter C. Welsh, *American Folk Art: The Art and Spirit of a People* (Washington, 1965), see also *Curator,* X:1 (1967), pp. 60-78; and Mary Black and Jean Lipman, *American Folk Painting* (New York, 1966), see also *Art in America,* 54:6 (November-December, 1966), pp. 113-128.

[22] The work of the Scot, Willie Robbie, is interesting in that it is, while not pop, not traditional; his creations, however, may be the source of a Lowland tradition which could be or become folk; see Kenneth S. Goldstein, "William Robbie: Folk Artist of the Buchan District, Aberdeenshire," in Horace P. Beck, ed., *Folklore in Action: Essays for Discussion in Honor of MacEdward Leach* (Philadelphia, 1962), pp. 101-111.

[23] Allen Eaton in *Rural Handicrafts in the United States* (Washington, 1946), p. 8.

[24] One of the best of the many discussions on this point by art critics and designers can be found in the third chapter of David Pye's *The Nature of Design* (New York, 1967).

[25] See particularly the preface and foreword to José E. Espinosa, *Saints in the Valleys* (Albuquerque, 1967).

[26] *The Shape of Time* (New Haven, 1962), pp. 14-16.

[27] For some material on the decoy see, Joel Barber, *Wild Fowl Decoys* (New York, 1954); Eugene V. Connett, *Duck Decoys* (New York, 1953); David S. Webster and William Kehoe, *Decoys at Shelburne Museum* (Shelburne, 1961); William J. Mackey, Jr., *American Bird Decoys* (New York, 1965): C. A. Porter Hopkins, "Maryland Decoys and Their Makers," *The Maryland Conservation* XLII:6 (November-December, 1965), pp. 2-5; Adele Earnest, *The Art of the Decoy* (New York, 1965).

[28] Cf. Lura Beam, *A Maine Hamlet* (New York, 1957), p. 186.

[29] Much has been written on hex signs; this has almost all dealt with whether or not they have magical significance, a proposition which has been neither proved nor disproved; for examples, see: John Joseph Stoudt, *The Decorated Barns of Eastern Pennsylvania* (Plymouth Meeting, 1945); Louis J. Heizmann, " Are Barn Signs Hex Marks?," *Historical Review of Berks County,* XII:1 (October, 1946), pp. 11-14; Alfred L. Shoemaker, *Hex No!* (Lancaster, 1953), a pamphlet constantly reprinted with different names; Olive G. Zehner, "The Hills from Hamburg," *The Pennsylvania Dutchman,* IV:11

(February 1,1953), pp. 16, 13; August C. Mahr, "Origin and Significance of Pennsylvania Dutch Barn Symbols," in Dundes, *The Study of Folklore,* pp. 373-399; Elmer L. Smith and Mel Horst, *Hex Signs and Other Barn Decorations* (Witmer, 1965). The more important questions of the forms, colors, distributions, and aesthetic meanings of the hex signs have yet to be answered.

[30] Jürg Spiller, *Paul Klee* (New York, 1968), pp. 11-12.

[31] See Henry Howe, *Historical Collections of the Great West,* II (New York and Cincinnati, 1857), pp. 190-194.

[32] by Rev. Walter Hughson (Hartford, 1908).

[33] by Harry M. Caudill (Boston, 1963).

[34] See Henry Glassie, "The Types of the Southern Mountain Cabin," in Jan H. Brunvand, *The Study of American Folklore* (New York, 1968), pp. 338-370.

[35] First published in 1903, this book was recently reprinted by the University of Nebraska Press.

[36] *Lou Rawls Live!*,Capitol S. T. 2459, side one, bands 2-3.

[37] A little on the skipjack can be found in M. V. Brewington, *Chesapeake Bay: A Pictorial Maritime History* (New York, 1956), pp. 65-66, 102-106.

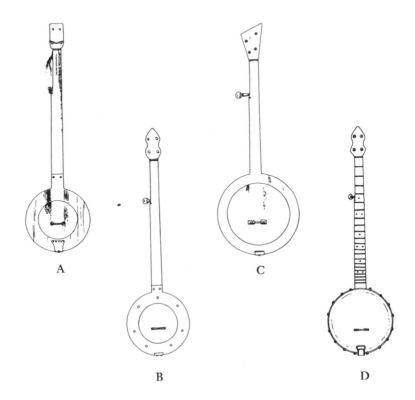

A   C

B   D

FIGURE 1

FIVE-STRING BANJOES
MADE IN THE SOUTHERN MOUNTAINS

A. Mack Presnell's "old piece of a banjer," made by Leonard Glenn about 1947, west of Sugar Grove, Watauga County, North Carolina (July, 1963). B. Curly maple, fretless banjo, made by Leonard Glenn in 1963, west of Sugar Grove, Watauga County, North Carolina (June, 1963). C. Cherry, fretless banjo, made by Edd L. Presnell in 1962, near Banner Elk, Watauga County, North Carolina (October, 1962). D. Bracket banjo with flush, inlaid frets made by Leonard Glenn in 1964, west of Sugar Grove, Watauga County, North Carolina (August, 1964).

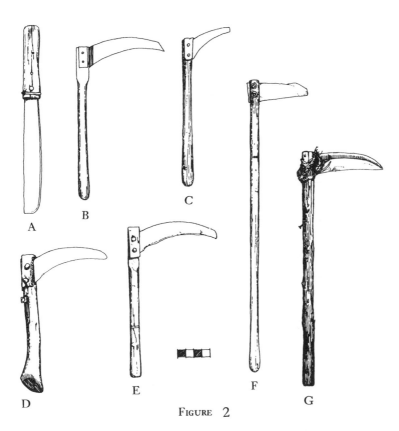

FIGURE 2

CORN KNIVES

A. Southwest of Tappahannock, Essex County, Virginia (August, 1966).
B. From *American Agriculturist*, XXVII:10 (October, 1868), p. 395.
The scale does not apply to this example. C. Near Dwight, Hampshire
County, Massachusetts (August, 1966). D. Between Lisbon and Hart-
wick, Otsego County, New York (July, 1965). E. East of South Ed-
meston, Otsego County, New York (November, 1964). F. South of
Orchid, Louisa County, Virginia (August, 1966). G. West of Orchid,
Louisa County, Virginia (August, 1966).

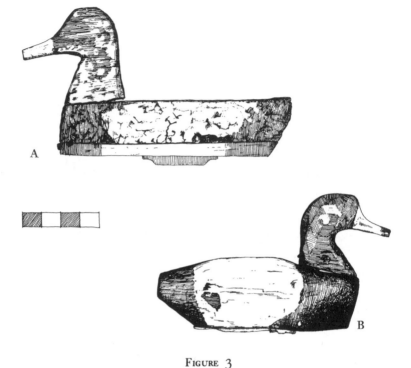

FIGURE 3

DUCK DECOYS

A. Cork bluebill decoy, Cape Hatteras, Dare County, North Carolina. B. Wooden bluebill decoy, Currituck Sound, Currituck County, North Carolina. Both are from the private collection of T. W. Sandoz, Chevy Chase, Maryland. The suppliers of hunting equipment (Herter's Catalog, 77 [Waseca, Minn., 1967], pp. 4–16) maintain "a complete testing laboratory," keep abreast of "scientific tests by some of the country's leading ornithologists," and tell the hunter that he must have a decoy with "every feather, muscle, and detail molded in"; still, Mr. Sandoz, with many years as a hunter behind him, said of these decoys: "The ducks will sit down to something like that. I've seen it many a time. They'll come up and peck it on the bill. . . . They're crude but they'll do the job" (August 20, 1967).

EXIT

by

Ray B. Browne

EXIT

by

Ray B. Browne

If there is one single characteristic of constancy in
present-day American society it is that of fluid chaos. In a time long
ago strikingly like ours John Donne voiced the general confusion:

And new Philosophy calls all in doubt,
The element of fire is quite put out;
The sun is lost, and the earth, and no man's wit
Can well direct him where to look for it.
And freely men confess that this world's spent,
When in the planets, and the firmament
They seek so many new; then see that this
Is crumbled out again to his atomies.

'Tis all in pieces, all coherence gone;
All just supply, and all relation:
Prince, subject, Father, Son, are things forgot.

Our new Philosophy is, of course, Technocracy. "The old order
changeth, yielding place to new," Tennyson observed in another
revolutionary period. When the new order intruding itself is as
unprecedented and far-reaching as unbridled technology, the effect
is bound to be shattering, to arouse terror and hostility,and the
resulting reaction causes many customs, mores, traditions and gods
to tumble.

Though this dawning Age of Aquarius is consequently one o
widespread and indiscriminate iconoclasm, paradoxically the general
power of icons to attract and hold the feelings of man has not really
diminished. Man's basic nature does not change so rapidly, if at all.
Temples and statues are not all removed overnight—or from one style
season to the next—but the accelerated process of revolutionary
change is at work. Many icons these days are made more of soap
than of stone, and the torrential beating waters wash many of them
away and change the shape of others. Yet the niches in which they
rest remain, and when they are made empty are refilled.

There are, of course, many waves washing the niches
today. The greatest is technocracy, which because of its very
nature causes this age to suffer more than any previous period from
the currents and counter-currents which charge and shock our culture
even to the brink of annihilation. As Wordsworth observed a hundred
and sixty years ago, the world is too much with us, and as he said he
would prefer to do, many of us have gone pagan and turned into
protesters.

Our protest works on many levels. On the most obvious
level there is the rebellion of flaming youth, flexing muscles and
employing tactics that make them an enraged Samson in Gaza, often
as eyeless and as destructive as he was. Read the words written in
fire—fittingly echoing the earlier great iconoclast Tom Paine—blazing
from one of their manifestoes:

The revolution which is beginning will call in
question not only capitalist society but industrial
society. The consumer's society must perish of a
violent death. The society of alienation must
disappear from history. We are inventing a new
and original world. Imagination is seizing power.[1]

Many youth thus demonstrate that they realize that present conditions of life are not what they want, that changes must be made.
Often this means, in their minds, merely tearing down the Establishment so that—hopefully—something better can be built on the ruins.

Another, smaller segment of youth is rebelling in yet another
way, with different tactics, though they too feel the same desperate
need. According to Theodore Roszak, these youngsters hold their
grudge with "technocracy's essential criminality: the extent to which
it insists, in the name of progress, in the name of reason, that the
unthinkable become thinkable and the intolerable become tolerable."
The youth of this group, however, assert "that healthy instinct which
refuses both at the personal and political level to practice such a
cold-blooded rape of our human sensibilities."[2]

In many ways one of the most thoughtful currents in the
rebellion against the shocking sixties and seventies has been, and
apparently will continue to be, among these thoughtful persons
who see man being forced into the electric chair by the computer
which controls every moment of our lives. These people—maybe
infants crying blindly in the wilderness, perhaps true prophets—feel
that because man is on the brink of total self-destruction the very
nature of *homo sapiens* is about to undergo a fundamental change,
that man is now on the threshold of a Renaissance that will make
the earlier period of the same name seem the simplest growing pains.
To such a critic as Ihab Hassan, as to many others, "Revolution is
no longer radical enough." Complete transformation of human
consciousness is demanded and possible. According to Hassan,
"Silence is perhaps the action we need to alter consciousness. Silence
is the means."[3]

In this the most technologically sophisticated and iconoclastic

of ages, paradoxically icon-worship has almost reached saturation
and turned to near idolatry. Now when the new philosophy calls
all things into doubt strange new gods are being created. Man's
nature demands, apparently, things to worship—icons, idols—to fill
an otherwise unfillable void. This is to a large extent youth's insistence
that the technocratic world they have been handed by their elders
is all mechanism and no soul, thus their desire to short-circuit the
computer and restore the supremacy of feeling. In trying to sabotage
the machine, people turn to strange new icons and idols.

Icons flash before us with psychedelic dazzling speed and
colors: LSD, marijuana and other drugs, long hair and dirty, slouchy
bodies and clothes, the motorcycle and souped-up automobile, etc.—
ESP, astrology, magic, mysticism, occultism, lines in the hand, witches,
the zodiac, utopianism, Charles Manson leading his group of hippies
in California, Anton Szandor LaVey holding services in the Church
of Satan in San Francisco. The number is legion.

Icons stretch the thread of existence from the blindest faith—
the statue of Christ on the dashboard of the speeding automobile
(what a juxtaposition is that!) to the most blatant snobbery—the
current advertisement for the Buick automobile (surely one of the
most vulgar mixtures of snobbishness and God) as "Something to
believe in."

Regardless of the lasting quality of these many icons—all or
some—each is a part of our present culture. They race upon us in
such numbers and speed that only a photographer working with a
high-speed lens can picture them all, let alone understand them.
But all represent our popular culture because all icons are in one
sense popular culture.

To observe a few of these, and to stimulate further study is
the purpose of this book. The limitations of this symposium are
apparent and recognized. It is (in the McLuhan sense) a probe. To
suggest that the ancient concept of "icon" deserves wider dimensions
than usually accorded it, we have advanced it further than some
people would allow, in directions which others will reject. Even
those people who concede that there are pop icons will raise questions
of typology, relationship of sacred and secular, confusions of fads

and trends, accuracy of implied iconography. We leave to later scholarship the task of separating species of icons and of differentiating them from emblems, amulets and idols. The task as we have developed it here is not so much to settle questions and categories as to raise them. This volume is not, then, a column of fire announcing the conclusion of a campaign but puffs of smoke broadcasting an appeal to observers to look all around them and to recognize and study these interesting and significant aspects of life.

NOTES

[1] From *The Times* (London), May 17, 1968: Edward Mortimer's report from Paris. Quoted in Theodore Roszak, *The Making of a Counter Culture* (New York, 1969), p. 22.

[2] Roszak, p. 47.

[3] Ihab Hassan, "Silence, Revolution, and Consciousness," *The Massachusetts Review,* Summer, 1969, pp. 469, 474.

2 shapes known the world over.

Nobody really notices Coke bottles or Volkswagens any more.

They're so well known, they blend in with the scenery.

It doesn't matter what the scenery is, either. You can walk in and buy a VW in any one of 136 countries. And that takes in lots of scenery.

Deserts. Mountains. Hot places. Cold places. Volkswagens thrive.

Hot and cold don't matter; the VW engine is air-cooled. It doesn't use water, so it can't freeze up or boil over.

And having the engine in the back makes all the difference when it comes to mud and sand and snow.

The weight is over the power wheels and so the traction is terrific.

VWs also get along so well wherever they are because our service is as good in Tasmania as it is in Toledo. (The only reason you can't buy a Volkswagen at the North Pole is that we won't sell you one. There's no VW service around the corner.)

We hear that it's possible to buy yourself a Coke at the North Pole, though.

Which makes us suspect there's only one thing that can get through ahead of a Volkswagen.

A Coke truck.

LEFT NUT: THE 1957 CHEVROLET

by

David Holwerk

LEFT NUT: THE 1957 CHEVROLET

by

David Holwerk

To set the record straight at the beginning: Though I have been
a longtime admirer and observer of the 1957 Chevrolet, I have never
owned one. My family at one point owned a 1958 Chevy station
wagon which was the first car I learned to drive, but that is the closest
I have ever come to owning a '57. Not very close, admittedly, but in
the part of the country where I grew up (that is to say, where I
reached puberty and got my driver's license) you got to know and
appreciate the machine for what it was worth whether you owned one
or not.

I am talking now of an appreciation which is more than a mechanics appreciation for a fine machine or a simple covetting of a sharp
car. There is an actual aesthetic built around the '57 Chevy, an aesthetic in every way as complete and sound (if less articulated) as any
penned by an artistic polemicist. This automotive aesthetic is, moreover, not merely a formulation or a piece of idle rumination. It is a

concrete ethic, as tangible in the actions of men as any principle I have ever encountered. Though its roots are deep and complex, its effect is widespread:

A 1957 Chevrolet is, to my knowledge, the only car which any-one has actually tried to save from being used in a demolition derby. At a derby in Louisville last year in which I drove, five people tried to dissuade another driver from entering his '57; each offered to buy the car from its owner, though it was in very poor condition, be-cause as one said, "Shit fire, man, you can't go crashing up one of them. Hell, she's got three or four good years left." Though there were many cars of similar vintage entered in the event, there was only the lone '57 Chevy and I was told that they are rare entries. "'57's is too valuable for this business," one track official explained. There was a feeling of sadness in the pits when the '57 went on the track, and nobody spoke to its driver when he was towed away with the front and rear of his car soundly demolished.

This reluctance to subject the '57 to demolition derbies is telling of its esteem among men who make their living out of cars. Almost everybody who drives in these car smashes is a mechanic or garage man, and there is more than a bit of catharsis involved in their efforts to destroy as many cars as they can with their own vehicle. One's relationship to his car is ambivalent at best, and it is seemingly true that the more you deal with the damn things, the more you want to smash hell out of them. But hardly anybody wants to destroy a '57 Chevy, proof in itself that the car is something special in the annals of Detroit.

It is impossible, really, to talk about the '57 without first talking about the '55 and the '56. One reason for the enduring success of the '57 is that the '55 was a completely new model, totally redesigned from the '54 Chevy. The '54 was not a bad car in its own right, but it was a little boxy and slow even for its day. The '55 changed Chev-rolet's reputation with longer, lower styling, new suspension, and im-proved automatic transmission and a new V-8 engine.

The styling and engine were the heart of the new model. The clean lines of the '55 Chevy made it an immediate favorite and now appear almost classic compared to the design of its contemporaries. The new engine, with 265 inches of piston displacement, was one of the most powerful in its class. *Popular Mechanics*, October, 1955, declared, "Chevrolet, once for conservative Charlies, sheds its image with new styling and power!" The '55 had a curb weight of 3125 pounds, a length of 195 inches and a 115 inch wheelbase. Twin airplane ornaments graced its hood and (powered by the 265 V-8) it would attain a top speed of 103 miles per hour.

The '55 was an excellent automobile, well designed and durable, but the '56 was even better. The 265 V-8 had already proven itself a fine engine, due in large measure to its short stroke piston design which added perhaps 20% to its life expectancy. For the 1956, however, the engine was refined with new rings and seals successfully combatting its original tendency to use oil. Although the wheelbase remained at 115 inches, the whole car was lengthened to 198 inches and the height lowered from 62.1 to 60.5 inches. The general lines remained the same, though the rear fender began to take on a more slightly finned appearance; the tail light assembly retained the basic inset, triangular shape of the '55, but was enlarged and opened. Although the car was heavier than its predecessor (3190-3310 lbs., depending on equipment), the 265's improvements allowed it to reach a speed of 108 m.p.h.

The '57 was a nearly perfect automobile. For one thing, the same general running gear which had been used on the '55 and refined on the '56 was sharpened still further on the '57. The design of the suspension and transmission, the steering and brakes, the rear end and electrical system was as nearly perfect as mass-produced machinery can be. Perhaps equally important, however, the '57 introduced a new engine to the world: The 283 V-8, built on the now-famous 265 block.

Because it was based on the 265, the 283 had none of the first year problems which usually mark new engines. The 283 was, if anything, even more dependable than the 265, and its added power pushed the car to speeds of 118 m.p.h.

The 283 was to become a classic in later years as the most dependable V-8 in Detroit history. Its dependability was in large measure due to the simplicity of its design, something which it shared with the rest of the '57. It is this simplicity, in fact, which has allowed the '57 to endure past all its competitors. I have been unable to obtain figures on how many '57's are still on the road, but informal surveys would indicate that there must be at least seven or eight times more of them on the road than Fords or Plymouths of similar vintage. There would also appear to be an equally greater number of '57 Chevies on the road than cars of later vintage. This is partly due to the fact that the '57 Chevy was produced in great volume (1,522,549), but few cars can match its record for durability and longevity.

The styling of the '57 was another factor in its favor. The basic design of the '55 and '56 is still visible in the '57, though there were changes. The tendency towards fins on the rear was now quite pronounced, and the triangulad tail light assembly had been done away with. The grille was more massive and stately and the car was lowered and lengthened. The *Popular Mechanics* Readers Report on the '57 Chevy (February, 1957) found that most of the owners liked their car's styling and power. Yet the great majority (three out of five) named cheap upkeep, sturdiness, and dependability as the '57's outstanding features.

So there were a lot of them made and they have lasted a long time. Their mere presence is enough to account for the value placed on them, one would think. And yet; and yet, well, no, it's not nearly enough. Though the 1957 Chevrolets are still sturdy and dependable, they are no longer prized simply for their utilitarian aspects. They are now a piece of popular art, a symbol of aspiration and hope not unlike the primitive art of any people. They are a statement about a part of this culture which is inexorably dying as the various problems and hazards of the individual automobile slowly leave little choice but to do away with cars altogether.

1957 might as well have been a hundred years ago now, for all the similarity it bears to today. It is foolish and pointless to glorify the fifties, but it is certainly no exaggeration to state that the world seemed to be put together more securely then. The biggest news story of the year was Elvis' induction into the Army. There were no interstate highways, few freeways, and the open road still held the possibility of something new at its end. We know what's at the end of the open road now: a city. And it's not really very open anyway, though you can drive faster than you could before. The road may have never held any promise, but that's a myth of this country which dies hard. For the ability to move on, the faith that there's a better place just a walk or a wagon ride or a drive away is integral to the history of this nation.

The automobile you know as well as you know the

slouch of the accumstomed body at the wheel,

James Agee wrote, discussing the Great American Roadside.

> You know the sweat and the steady throes of the
> motor and the copious and thoughtless silence and
> the almost lack of hunger and the spreaded swell
> and swim of the hard highway toward and beneath
> and behind and gone and the parted roadside swarm-
> ing past . . . Oh, yes, you know this talk at the gas
> station, the welcome taste of a Bar-B-Q sandwich in
> midafternoon, the oddly excellent feel of a weak-
> springed bed in a transient shack, and the early start
> in the cold, bright, lonesome air, the dustless and
> dewy road . . .

Well, maybe we still know that road, but not intimately. We remember it, perhaps, or we are told of it, but we don't travel on it much
any more. There is no sweat in air conditioned cars, no throes of
the motor audible in the insulated privacy of the front seat. The gas
station runs on credit cards and we know only the oddly unpleasant
rest of a Holiday Inn bed. We only get in the car now because we
know where we are going, and there is always a four-lane road to
take us there. And if there is no four-lane road, then we'll get a
four-wheel drive camper and make our own, by God.

The death of the open road, the great American highway to
happiness, must eventually signal the death of the automobile, as the
great symbol of success and status in our society. For as the pleasure
in driving decreases, the impetus for owning a snazzy car must go
with it. Auto makers try like hell, of course, with all variety of
muscle and compact cars to revive the enthusiasm which the nation
once had for cars, but I fear they will meet with little success. Driving and owning cars is just too much of a pain these days, and anyway, where's there to go? Although we may buy more cars this year
than ever before, we are enjoying and believing in them less and that
is a dangerous position for any myth.

So owning a '57 Chevy now is more than owning a car. It is a
declaration of hope, albeit to something which is past. Sure, some
people own a '57 because they got it cheap somewhere, but that is a
thing whose day is done, too. There are no cheap cars, no good deals
any more. If you believe that you can get a sharp deal on a set of

wheels, then you implicitly understand the attraction of a '57 Chevy: For fifteen years it has been the sharpest deal around.

But what will happen to all those people who still believe in the car and the deal? What will replace it as a standard of faith and constancy? The open road is gone forever, and with it a lot of things we all took for granted as rights and opportunities. The '57 Chevy can't go on forever, nor can it restore the road to us. The best we can hope for is that we can keep them out of the demolition derbies for a few more years, while we look for a new way of getting wherever it is that we are going.

It is a very clever ad when the Man From Allstate says, "Let's make driving a GOOD THING again!" For it is more than a pointless slogan to want to do just that. It is actually a desire which is at the heart of our current set of dilemmas. (Pick your favorite.) Things are so out of control that—incredible as it sounds—even driving has gone to pot. It's a sad state of affairs, and if I thought it would help, nothing would stand between me and a '57 Chevy. My heart is with those who would save these proud machines from the demolition derbies, but I confess that I fear even the '57's will be of little help to us now. As long as I see them on the road, though, some small part of me will always think, "Now, there's a hell of a car." Where once I would have given my left nut to own one, now I would give it just to believe in one again.

BOTTOMS UP: PLACE NAMES ON COKE BOTTLES

by

Sylvia Grider

BOTTOMS UP: PLACE NAMES ON COKE BOTTLES

by

Sylvia Grider

Reading place names on the bottomsof Coke bottles is as much
a part of my upbringing as are the now defunct Burma Shave signs.
But like so many aspects of our industrialized society, these names
are disappearing, under ecological stress,[1] in direct proportion to the
pop top can and throw-away bottle, which one buys out of the Coke
machine now for 15 cents instead of a nickel. Inflation and progress
have attacked yet another of our well known popular icons.[2] However, as long as Volkswagen can successfully advertise, "Two shapes
known the world over," illustrated by a VW and a Coke bottle, there
must still be hope.[3]

   We still have multi-media advertising phenomena as remarkable
as the *I'd Like to Buy the World a Coke* song, "filmed on a hilltop
in Italy," featuring the classic, 6½ ounce Coca Cola bottle. Craig
Gilborn has provided us with a very thorough classification system

and interpretation of the Coke bottle. Before discussing the place names on the bottoms of the bottles and their many interpretations and uses, let us first put the Coke in cultural context.

While on excavation in Ancient Corinth, Greece, we often used to laugh about what an upheaval of ancient chronology we would cause if an ancient pottery Coke bottle should emerge. Such joking inevitably made us all achingly thirsty for a Coke, but alas, there was no Coke franchise in Greece at that time. The local soft drink, Tam-Tam, tried to seduce American tourists with its Coke-like bottle and beverage color but popular demand won out. Coca Cola has returned to modern Greece.

I soon discovered that our association of the Coke bottle with archeological stratification was by no means a unique idea. Gilborn suggests using Coke bottles to teach students to "develop an awareness of the diverse attributional character of objects" in creating classification systems.[4] And F. Clark Howard in *Early Man* says, "Since the oldest stone implements that could possibly be recognized as such today are only about two million years old, we must assume that practically all of the ones that have ever been made are still lying around somewhere or other. It is not surprising that a good many of them have been found, any more than it would be surprising for some archeologist of the future to stumble over a quantity of Coca Cola bottles sleeping quietly where they had been dropped, one by one, into the ooze beneath the pier of a waterside pavillion. Every culture leaves some odds and ends behind, many of them very long-lived."[5] A salient example of this longevity bears direct relation to the Coke-archeology analogy. At the height of the Hellenistic trade period of antiquity, the Greeks stamped the handles of their pottery amphorae with the place of origin of the wine within.[6] The place names on the bottoms of Coke bottles have a distinguished ancestry. A colleague of mine once whiled away a whole class period reconstructing twentieth century culture through the eyes of the archeologist of the future via the Coke bottle.[7] They conjectured a female cult worshipping society (note the hourglass, female form of the bottle and the feminine inflected ending of Coca Cola) which offered libations to its goddess in these bottles, which are found all over the world . . . and so on as far as the imagination will stretch.

These archeological mental meanderings make their own comments about our society; namely the Coke bottle is universally recognized and accepted as an integral part of those "things" which lend us stability in a seemingly ever-changing world. Raymond Lowey, a noted industrial who designed the first streamlined train and the 1953 Studebaker, said that other than the egg, the classic 6½ ounce Coke bottle is the world's most perfectly designed package. He noted specifically the feminine form of the bottle and that it is the ideal shape for the hand to grasp—a commentary on the merger of aesthetics and function.[8]

But how does something as mundane as a soft drink bottle stabilize our attitudes toward ourselves? What is the cultural context into which it fits? What traditions do we have which are inextricably bound up with the Coke bottle specifically, without special emphasis on the tremendous amount of oral material regarding the "secret" Coca Cola formula and where it is hidden or the recurring joke cycles about the beverage and associated advertising slogans?

The first context is that great American ritual, the Coke break, sometimes known as the coffee break. Throughout the country, working people and housewives take time off at mid-morning and mid-afternoon to "have a Coke" and relax a few minutes before resuming work. Semantically this is of interest because in this case "Coke" becomes synonymous with whatever one chooses to drink during the break. The evening pastime of teenagers of "going out to get a Coke" amounts to about the same thing. In the 1940's the Andrews Sisters extolled *Drinking Rum and Coca Cola* and later the jingle could be heard on the radio or seen on billboards, "Fifty million times a day, at home, at work, or on the way, there's nothing like a Coca Cola, nothing like a Coke." After progressing through innumerable advertising slogans such as, "Things go better with Coke," or, "It's the real thing," we have the currently popular *I'd Like to Buy the World a Coke* with all its variants.

Coke has found its way from music into our oral tradition too. When I was a teenager, "Jinks, you owe me a Coke," was the immediate response or incantation to break the hex whenever two people made the same remark simultaneously. And "dope" used to be the nickname for Coke, possibly because of its phonetic similarity to cocaine, before narcotics abuse became such a problem in this country. Jan Brunvand dug up a *blason populaire* on the Coke, "What do they print on the bottoms of Coke bottles in Kentucky? Open other end."9

In 1961 the United Artists comedy *One, Two, Three*, starring James Cagney and produced by Billy Wilder, dealt with the traumas of the Coca Cola franchise in East and West Berlin. Coke seemed to be the only universal medium through which audiences could comically approach and reconcile the international tensions that were building up at that time over the Berlin Wall.

In the realm of literature, after the nuclear holocaust in Nevil Shute's *On the Beach*, it is an errant Coke bottle that taps the telegraph key whenever the wind blows and thus sends what is believed to be a signal from the last living American to the rest of the devastated world. Appropriate enough.10

There are still other customs associated with Coke bottles. Americans travelling abroad have a penchant for bringing home Coke bottles from foreign countries. Especially popular are those with the brand name in Arabic or Japanese. Here the American is recognizing a reflection of himself in other cultures. This fancy for souvenirs plus the vast foreign student enrollment at Indiana University caused quite a problem when the local Firestone store offered a cash prize of $50 "for the person bringing in Coke bottle farthest distance from Bloomington; look on bottom of bottle."11 The store manager said that this particular advertising contest had never been held in a college town before and they were not expecting the avalanche of foreign bottles that were brought in. Although he couldn't remember exactly what country they were from, the contest money was finally split between the owners of two bottles with the brand name in Arabic.12

The collectors' market has also zeroed in on the Coke bottle. The "Christmas Bottle" is currently one of the most popular. It has "Bottle Pat'd. Dec. 25, 1923" embossed just beneath the brand name. Almost any antique dealer will tell you that since the U. S. patent office is not open on Christmas day, this is undoubtedly a *rare* item. The Christmas Bottle is consequently listed in many antique catalogues at varying prices. In fact, the owner of an antique shop in Nashville, Indiana, said that "antique" Coke bottles have become so popular that a special dealer from Atlanta, Georgia, comes in every spring with a new stock of old bottles.13

When I was an undergraduate at the University of Texas, there was a story that there was a fellow in the Anthropology Department who could chip perfect arrowheads out of Coke bottles using a deer antler as a tool. This may or may not have been true, but I also remember my own father telling me that when he was a Boy Scout chipping arrowheads from Coke bottles was a popular pastime on camping trips. Do Boy Scouts still do this?

But the main body of tradition associated with Coke bottles deals with the games people play based on the place names on the bottoms of the bottles.

The original purpose of marking the bottoms of the bottles, as with the ancient wine amphorae, was to indicate the town in which the product was bottled. However, since Coke bottles are interchangeable and filled on a mechanized assembly line, these place names no longer hold any such significance. The glass factories ship whatever they have in stock to whichever of the approximately 800 bottlers in the U. S. needs them, with no regard to the place names on the bottles. But this fact makes no difference to those who play the games associated with the place names.

Between 1958-1960, when the trademark first began to be painted on the bottles instead of embossed, many factories produced bottles with blank bottoms because they were cheaper. By 1963 public demand caused the Coca Cola Company to have the glass manufacturers resume embossing place names on the bottles, using whatever dies they had available. Coke did this, ". . . so that our customers may employ them in harmless games with their friends, and as an aid in hobby collecting."[14]

Since the bottles with which we are concerned have both the date and place name on them, the logical approach is the historic-geographic method. However, I emphasized the geographic and virtually ignored the historic aspect. I compiled a list of names on 100 bottles each from Pampa, Texas, and Bloomington, Indiana. 100 was an arbitrary, random sample number. A larger sample might produce more conclusive results. All of the bottles I read in Pampa were at the Coca Cola Bottling Plant. Those in Bloomington were from the National Guard Armory and Hatch's I. G. A., both of which are supplied by the Cloomington Coca Cola Bottling Plant.

Pampa and Bloomington are similar in many respects. Both have relatively stable populations of approximately 35,000 and neither is located directly on a main national highway or Interstate but instead is about 50 miles from one. The main difference and factor of variability is that I. U. with more than 30,000 highly transient students is located in Bloomington.

"Whoever gets the bottle from farthest away wins," is the main game associated with Coke place names. What is won is immaterial. Sometimes at Coke break whoever gets the bottle from farthest away has to pay for the Cokes of the rest of the group; or it can be just the opposite. A popular way to entertain children on long auto trips is to play a variant. When the driver stops to gas up, the child who gets the "farthest" bottle from the Coke machine wins, sometimes just winning for the sake of winning or maybe getting a chance to sit in the front seat until the next stop. Such cross country travelling seems to be the main way that Coke bottles get so randomly distributed across the country. We Americans are in such a hurry that few stay at the service station long enough to finish. We take bottles to turn in as a deposit on another somewhere else on down the road— and so on countless times a day over the years until the bottles wander back and forth across the country. I remember learning the abbreviations of the states by reading them on the bottles and asking Mother about those I didn't know. It is also fun to get a bottle out of the machine from some obscure town nobody in the group has ever heard of and then try to guess where in the particular state that town may be located. The enterprising end up by consulting a map or atlas.

This fascination with "the bottle from farthest away" exists among all strata of our society. When the janitor at the Coke plant in Pampa finally figured out what I was doing looking at all those bottles, he came over to help me and ended up telling me about the bottles that he had seen. The plant once got a bottle from Japan and he was fascinated by the fact that "it just didn't look like ours. It was all milky white and the lettering was funny, but you could tell she was a Coke bottle all right."15 He also mentioned a bottle they found one day, "All the way from London, England. But it was so beat up you couldn't hardly read the writing on it no more."

As a rule American bottlers do not refill foreign bottles because they are clear glass instead of the familiar standard green. American throw-aways, with "Not to be refilled" embossed on the bottom, are also clear. Mexico has turned out to be an exception. Mexican bottles are green and indistinguishable from American ones except for on the label beneath the trademark is painted, in Spanish, "Marca Reg. Mexico, D. F.," and "Hecho en Mexico." There is no name on the bottom. Occasionally one of these slips past the inspector and gets rebottled in the U. S. I encountered my first on in Hearne, Texas. The waitress couldn't decide whether to charge me extra for the bottle since it was foreign (she apparently wanted it too) so we settled on a nickel as a fair price and I got my first foreign Coke bottle.

But now, to the geographic distribution of the bottles. Are the bottles in Bloomington, excluding the foreign ones, more widely diffused than those in Pampa?

In Pampa twenty-one states and sixty-one towns were represented; in Bloomington, twenty-five states and sixty-five towns. In Pampa over half the bottles (fifty-one) were from Texas, but taking into consideration that the size of Texas is roughly equivalent to Illinois, Indiana, Ohio, Michigan, West Virginia, and Kentucky, all contiguous states and that they produced forty-three bottles as opposed to Texas' fifty-one, it makes it difficult to support an argument that Bloomington bottles are from farther away. Still Pampa had eight local bottles and Bloomington's sample produced only two locals.

Based on this random sample, what conclusions can be drawn? We can only say that the Coca Cola bottle is ubiquitous and reflects the tremendous mobility of the American people. Coke bottles accompany us wherever we go. A flow chart of distribution would be impossible to develop, since the place names no longer bear any relation to where the bottle was originally filled. The pop top can, throw-aways, and the fact that people have an increasing tendency not to return the returnables anyway are combining to put a gradual end to the games and traditions associated with reading Coke bottle bottoms. Nevertheless, the bottle itself, especially the classic 6½ ounce, is still with us after over fifty years of manufacture, remarkable both for its uniformity and subtle differences. Hopefully the demand of the American public will keep some of them around for years to come.

NOTES

[1]"The Return of the Returnables?" *Time.* Vol. 96. Sept. 21, 1970. pp. 70-71.

[2]Gilborn, Craig. "Pop Iconology: Looking at the Coke Bottle." *Icons of Popular Culture.* Bowling Green University Popular Press. 1970. p. 24.

146

[3]Rowsome, Frank. *Think Small. The Story of Those Volkswagen Ads.* Stephen Greene Press. Brattleboro, Vt. 1971. p. 31.

[4]Gilborn. *Op. cit.* p. 16.

[5]Howard F. Clark. *Early Man. Time/Life Nature Library.* New York. 1965. pp. 101-102.

[6]*Excavations of the Athenian Agora Picture Book No.6: Amphoras and the Ancient Wine Trade.* American School of Classical Studies at Athens. c/o Institute for Advance Study. Princeton, New Jersey.

[7]Robert Rossow to Sylvia Grider. Bloomington, Indiana. March 6, 1972.

[8]Bernard Lootens to Sylvia Grider. Telephone conversation. April 9, 1972. (Mr. Lootens is a Michigan City, Indiana, teacher who has maintained a long interest in Lowey and his work.)

[9]Brunvand, Jan. "Some Thoughts on Ethnic-Regional Jokes." *Indiana Folklore.* Vol. III, No. 1. 1970. p. 139.

[10]Shute, Nevil. *On the Beach.* William Morrow and Company. New York. 1967. p. 201.

[11]*Indiana Daily Student.* September 8, 1971.

[12]Tom Sander, Firestone Manager, to Sylvia Grider. Bloomington, Indiana. March 7. 1972.

[13]Kathy Hurlburt, owner, The Brown County Peddler, to Sylvia Grider. Nashville, Indiana. November 23, 1971.

[14]E. Blair Proctor, The Coca Cola Company, Atlanta, Georgia, to Sylvia Grider. Personal correspondence. March 15, 1972.

[15]Name of informant unknown. Pampa, Texas. January 7, 1972.

CONTRIBUTORS

Spencer C. Bennett is Instructor in Interdisciplinary Studies at Case-Western Reserve University. He is finishing his doctoral dissertation on transcendentalism, as well as cultivating his interest in religious themes in contemporary mass media.

Arthur Berger, associate professor at San Francisco State College, has recently published two pioneering studies in the field of popular culture: *Li'l Abner: A Study in American Satire* and *The Evangelical Hamburger*.

B. A. Botkin, one of the deans of American folklorists, lives in Croton-on-Hudson, New York, and is deeply engaged in studying the theory and practice of popular culture.

Nicholas Calas, is the author, among other works, of *Art in the Age of Risk and Other Essays* (New York, E. P. Dutton & Co., Inc. 1968).

Craig Gilborn, Director of the Delaware State Art Council, spent six years on the staff of the Winterthur Museum, where he was concerned with third dimensional history and icons.

Henry Glassie, who specializes in material folk culture, is on the faculty at the Folklore Institute, Indiana University.

Sylvia Grider is at Indiana University, Bloomington.

Harry Hammond, instructor in American Studies at the University of Delaware, drives the vehicle of which he speaks.

David Holwerk is Senior Resident Fellow at the Tolson Institute, Cincinnati, Ohio.

Marshall McLuhan directs the Centre of Technology and Culture at Toronto University. In the last decade he has become a cult figure in the Electronic Age and has identified many new icons.

Sam Rosenberg is a free-lance writer who lives on Long Island and writes in many journals about popular culture.

Fred Schroeder teaches at the Duluth campus of the University of Minnesota, where (he says) colleagues tell students to take his course—but not to take it seriously.

EDITORS

Ray B. Browne, professor of English and American Studies at Bowling Green University, is Director of the Center for the Study of Popular Culture and edits the *Journal of Popular Culture* and the Popular Press.

Marshall W. Fishwick, is professor of Art and History at Lincoln University and Director of the American Studies Institute.